Christine Al

W9-AVI-908

THE ANCIENT
CHINESE WORLD

RONALD MELLOR &
AMANDA H. PODANY
GENERAL EDITORS

THE ANCIENT CHINESE WORLD

Terry Kleeman & Tracy Barrett

OXFORD
UNIVERSITY PRESS

For Greg—T. B.
For Faye—T. K.

OXFORD
UNIVERSITY PRESS

Oxford New York
Auckland Bangkok Buenos Aires Cape Town Chennai
Dar es Salaam Delhi Hong Kong Istanbul Karachi Kolkata
Kuala Lumpur Madrid Melbourne Mexico City Mumbai
Nairobi São Paulo Shanghai Taipei Tokyo Toronto

Copyright © 2005 by Oxford University Press

Published by Oxford University Press, Inc.
198 Madison Avenue, New York, New York, 10016
www.oup.com

Oxford is a registered trademark of Oxford University Press

All rights reserved. No part of this publication may be reproduced,
stored in a retrieval system, or transmitted, in any form or by any means,
electronic, mechanical, photocopying, recording, or otherwise,
without the prior permission of Oxford University Press.

Design: Stephanie Blumenthal
Layout: Alexis Siroc
Cover design and logo: Nora Wertz

Library of Congress Cataloging-in-Publication Data

Kleeman, Terry F.
  The ancient Chinese world / by Terry Kleeman and Tracy Barrett.
    p. cm. — (World in ancient times)
  Audience: Ages 11–14.
    ISBN-13: 978-0-19-517102-0 -- 978-0-19-522246-3 (Calif. ed.) -- 978-0-19-522242-5 (set)

1. China—History—To 221 B.C. 2. China—History—Qin dynasty, 221–207 B.C. 3. China—History—
Han dynasty, 202 B.C.–220 A.D. I. Barrett, Tracy II. Title. III. Series.
DS741.5.K55 2004
931—dc22

                                                                2004014408

9 8 7 6 5 4 3

Printed in the United States on acid-free paper.

On the cover: A terracotta tambourine player from the Han dynasty.
Frontispiece: A jade amulet from the Shang dynasty.

RONALD MELLOR &
AMANDA H. PODANY

GENERAL EDITORS

CONTENTS

CAST OF CHARACTERS

In Chinese, the family name comes first, so that is how we alphabetized this list. Also, emperors and kings are listed under the name of the country that they ruled.

Andersson, Johan Gunnar, 1874–1960 • Swedish archaeologist who found Peking Man

Ban Zhao (bahn jaow), about 45–116 CE • Author of *Precepts for Women* and part of the *History of the Han*

Bao Si (baow suh), active 775 BCE • Wife of King You of Zhou whose whims contributed to her husband's downfall

Cao Cao (tsaow tsaow), 155–220 CE • General and poet who effectively ruled for the last 15 years of the Han dynasty

Chen She (chen shuh), d. 208 BCE • Leader of peasant revolt at end of Qin

Confucius (con-FYU-shus) or **Kong Qiu** (kong cheeoh), 551–479 BCE • China's first philosopher

Diviner Su (soo), active 676 BCE • Fortune teller to Duke Xian of Jin

Duke of Zhou (jo), active 1040 BCE • Younger brother of King Wu and regent to King Cheng

Feng Yan (fuhng yen), active 56 CE • Man who wrote a letter complaining about his wife and threatening divorce

Gao Xi (gow she), active 685 BCE • Former adviser to Duke Huan of Qi

Gautama, Siddharta (GOW-tam si-DARTH), about 460–380 BCE • The Buddha, or Enlightened One, founder of Buddhism

Gu Jiegang (goo jee-eh gahng), 1893–1980 • Modern Chinese scholar who discovered Yu the Great was a myth

Guan Zhong (gwahn jong), about 730–645 BCE • Able adviser to Duke Huan of Qi

Han (hahn) **dynasty** • Liu clan that ruled China from 202 BCE to 220 CE, with a brief interruption 9–23 CE

Hao (how), **Lady,** d. about 1200 BCE • Powerful Shang queen, wife of Wuding

Huhai (hoo-hi), ruled 209–207 BCE • Second emperor of Qin

Jia Lanpo (jeeah lahn-pwoh), 1908– 2001 • Modern Chinese archaeologist who excavated Peking Man

Jiang Yuan (jeeahng yewen) • Legendary ancestress of the Ji (jee) clan that ruled the Zhou

Jin (jeen) **dynasty** • Sima family that ruled all of China (265–316 CE), then just the South (317–420 CE)

Jin (jeen), **Duke Xian** (sheeahn) **of,** ruled 676–651 BCE • Ruler of the state of Jin, father of Shensheng

Jing Ke (jing kuh), d. 227 BCE • Assassin sent to kill Ying Zheng

Jiu (jeeoh), **Heir of Qi**, d. 685 BCE • Elder brother of Duke Huan of Qi, killed by him

Laozi (laow-dzuh) • Mythical author of *Daodejing* (daow-duh-jing)

Li (lee), **Lady,** of the Rong (roong), mid-seventh century BCE • Rong princess who married Duke Xian of Jin

Li Zhaodong (lee jaow-dong) • Man who may know the location of Peking man's bones

Liang (leeahng), **Emperor Wu** (woo) **of,** 464–549 CE, ruled 502–549 CE • Founder of Liang dynasty, great believer and patron of Buddhism

Liu Bang (leeoh bahng), ruled 206–196 BCE • Peasant founder of the Han dynasty

Liu Bei (leeoh bay), 162–223 CE • Relative of the Han royal house, founder of the state of Shu-Han in Sichuan

Liu Yuan (leeoh yewen), ruled 304–310 CE • Ruler of the Xiongnu tribe, founded a brief Han dynasty in the North

Mencius (men-shus) or **Meng Ke** (muhng kuh), about 370–290 BCE • Confucian philosopher

Mozi (mwoh-dzuh), about 470–390 BCE • Philosopher and founder of the Mohist school

Qi (chee), **Duke Huan** (hwahn) **of,** ruled 685–643 BCE • First hegemon

Qi (chee), **the Lord of Millet** • Legendary founder of the Ji clan and first to plant grain

Qin (chin) **dynasty** • Ying clan that ruled China from 221 to 206 BCE

Qin Shi Huangdi (chin shur hwahng-dee). See Ying Zheng.

Shang (shahng) **dynasty** • Clan that ruled from about 1500 to 1046 BCE

Shang (shahng), **King Di Xin** (dee shin) of, died 1046 BCE • Evil last king of the Shang dynasty

Shang (shahng), **King Wuding** (woo-ding) of, ruled around 1200 BCE • Most powerful Shang king

Shang Yang (shahng yahng), about 390–338 BCE • Prime Minister of Qin and Legalist reformer

Shensheng (shehn-shuhng), mid-seventh century BCE • Son of Duke Xian of Jin

Sima Qian (suh-ma cheeyen) about 145–86 BCE • China's most famous historian and author of *Record of the Historian,* a history of everything that happened in China up to his time

Sun Quan (swun chooen), 182–252 CE • founder of the state of Wu in southeast China

Sun Wu (swun woo), active 512 BCE • General and military strategist who wrote the *Art of War*

Wang Mang (wahng mahng), 45 BCE–23 CE • Ruled 9–23 CE; overthrew the Han dynasty and set up the Xin

Wei (way) **dynasty** • Cao family that ruled China from 220 to 265 CE

Xiang Yu (sheeahng yew), d. 203 BCE • General from Chu who fought with Liu Bang for the empire

Xiang Zhuang (sheeahng jwahng), active 206 BCE • Follower of Liu Bang, protects him in sword dance

Yi (yee), **Marquis** (mar-kee) **of Zeng** (dzehng), d. about 433 BCE • ruler of small state of Zeng

Ying Zheng (ing jehng), ruled 246–210 BCE • First emperor of Qin

Yu (yew) • Mythical tamer of great flood and founder of Xia dynasty

Zhang Ling (jahng ling), active 142 CE • Founder of Celestial Master Daoism who experienced revelation from Laozi

Zhang Lu (jahng loo), d. 215 CE • Organizer of the Celestial Masters who led their independent state; grandson of Zhang Ling

Zhao Gao (jaow gaow), d. 207 BCE • Qin general who installed Huhai as second emperor

Zhou (jo) **dynasty** • Ji clan that ruled China about 1045–221 BCE

Zhou (jo), **King Cheng** (chung) **of,** ruled 1042/1035–1006 BCE • Son of King Wu

Zhou (jo), **King Li** (lee) **of,** ruled 857–842 BCE • Cruel Western Zhou king whose people criticized him

Zhou (jo), **King Wen** (wun) **of,** ruled 1099–1050 BCE • Zhou king who was imprisoned by the Shang; later he plotted the Shang downfall

Zhou (jo), **King Wu** (woo) **of,** ruled 1050–1043 • Wen's son; led the armies of the west to conquer Shang

Zhou (jo), **King You** (yo) **of,** ruled 781–771 BCE • Last ruler of the Western Zhou

SOME PRONUNCIATIONS

Anyang (ahn-yahng)

Bo Hai (bwoh hi)

Chang'an (chahng-ahn)

Xi'an (shee-ahn)

Chengziyai (chehng-dzuh-yai)

Da Yi Shang (da yee shahng)

Song (soong)

Erlitou (ar-lee-tow)

Fen River (fuhn)

Gobi Desert (GO-bee)

Hemudu (huh-moo-doo)

Jin (jeen)

Manchuria (man-CHUR-ee-a)

Mongolia (mohn-GO-lee-a)

Qi (chee)

Qin (chin)

Quwo (choo-wo)

Sanzingdui (sahn-shing-dway)

Taklamakan Desert (tah-klah-mah-KAHN)

Yangshao (yahng-shaow)

Yangzi River (yahng-dzuh)

Zeng (dzeng)

MONGOLIA

Gobi Des

Taklamakan Desert

•Dunhuang

TIBET

Himalayas

INDIA

Bay of Bengal

THE ANCIENT CHINESE WORLD

Manchuria

Sea of Japan

KOREA

JAPAN

Bo Hai

Yellow Sea

Yan

Zhoukoudian
Cave ✕

ow River

Fen River

•Qi

Chengziyai

Xiaotun
✕ Anyang
•Jin

Da Yi Shang
(Song)

Chang'an
(Xi'an)
•Quwo

•Pei

•Zhengzhou

Pacific Ocean

Qin

Yangshao

Zeng

Hemudu ✕

CHINA

East China Sea

nxingdui

Three
Gorges

gzi River

Taiwan

South China Sea

IETNAM

0   400 mi

0   600 km

INTRODUCTION
THE CREATION OF THE UNIVERSE

The creator god Pangu wore branches because people were not around yet to invent clothing. In his left hand he holds a globe labeled "sun" and in his right hand one labeled "moon."

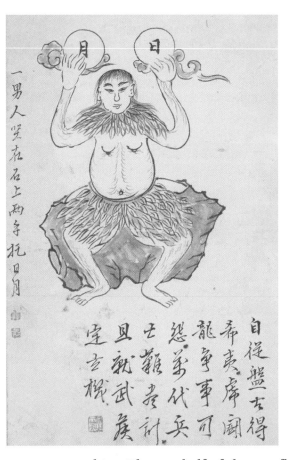

In the beginning, says a Chinese myth, the universe was contained in a huge black egg. Everything that eventually became the earth and the heavens swirled inside its enormous shell.

Something else was in the egg: the god Pangu, who managed to stay sound asleep for 18,000 years despite the crowded conditions. When he woke up he separated the different things inside the egg into opposing parts: male and female, light and dark, wet and dry, hot and cold. But Pangu kept growing and eventually he started to feel cramped, so he picked up an axe and broke the shell that was imprisoning him. The top half of the egg floated up to become the sky, and the bottom half fell, becoming the earth. Pangu kept growing, and his body pushed the sky and the earth farther and farther apart.

Immortal means living forever.

Although he was a god, Pangu was not **immortal** and eventually he died. His breath turned into the wind and the clouds, and his voice, according to legend, is still heard as thunder. The god's body became the earth's mountains and rivers, and his hair turned into stars. The fleas and lice living on his body became the ancestors of human beings.

In time, these people needed a ruler. Chinese tradition says that the founder of their first ruling family was a man named Yu. Yu was a miraculous person. Not only was he born from the dead body of his father, but he could change into a bear. He could also work harder than anyone else and once wore himself out so much by laboring for his people that his fingernails even stopped growing. He cut channels in the earth to change the course of mighty rivers to drain flood waters. Further proof of his unusual nature was that a nine-tailed fox predicted his marriage. Later, his wife ran away from him—she accidentally saw him in his bear shape and was understandably upset —and turned into stone. At the time, she was pregnant with a boy and Yu demanded that she give him his son, so the stone split open and the boy came out of it.

Of course, these tales are myths and nobody thinks they're literally true anymore. But some historians think that a great ruler, whose name might have been Yu or might have been something else, lived in China in the distant past and was so powerful that legends grew up around him. Scholars argue most about whether the Xia **dynasty**, which Yu supposedly founded, really existed.

THE GREAT FLOOD

Yu's most famous feat was saving his people from a devastating flood. The story goes that when the Yellow River overflowed its banks and threatened a large area, Yu worked for 13 years, digging valleys through the mountains. He was so busy that he passed by his own front door three times without stepping inside to say hello to his wife or to take a rest. Finally the excess water flowed through Yu's channels and the people were saved.

Many other cultures tell a story about a hero who saves his people from a flood. The Babylonian Utnapishtim, the Hebrew Noah, the Hindu Manu, the Aztec Tapi, and the Hawaiian Nuu are just a few examples from around the world.

The Chinese people have always had mixed feelings about the Yellow River. It is the primary source of water for northern China, but its flooding has killed thousands of people over the years.

{ A dynasty is a series of rulers from the same family.

GRAND HISTORIAN
SIMA QIAN

Sima Qian lived from about 145 BCE to about 86 BCE. He was a Grand Historian—the rulers of his time thought that the recording of history was so important that "Grand Historian" was a hereditary government position. Sima Qian's father, Sima Tan, had begun a great history of China, but it was unfinished at his death. Sima Qian completed it around 100 BCE as the *Record of the Historian.*

When he was young, Sima Qian visited historical sites across southern China and followed the Chinese army in its expeditions to the southwest, as far as modern Kunming. His job included not only making official records for the court but also keeping track of the movements of the stars and planets and other natural events that people thought could predict the future.

The earliest history book written in Chinese is the anonymous *Book of Documents,* parts of which were written about 1040 BCE. It's clear that the writers of the early speeches and proclamations contained in the book assume that the Xia existed. For instance, they mention the Xia's evil last ruler as a real person, not a legend.

Sima Qian, who wrote a later history called the *Record of the Historian* in about 100 BCE, uses older documents as sources and mentions the Xia. Some modern historians say that these accounts are just retellings of legends. But ancient Chinese historians thought Sima Qian's book was accurate, and, in fact, later writers modeled their own accounts of history on what he had written. Modern scholars who believe in the historical existence of the Xia point out that people used to think that the *Record of the Historian* was wrong about other things that were later found to be accurate. For instance, historians used to think that Sima Qian's lists of kings of the Shang dynasty, who ruled from about 1500 BCE to about 1046 BCE, were made up. Later, texts written on bones during the time of the Shang showed almost exactly the same list of kings. If the book was correct about this, why should we automatically assume that it's wrong about the Xia? Shouldn't we give its authors the benefit of the doubt?

Despite all the stories of King Yu's miracles, later Chinese artists always depicted him as a typical emperor. Yu's tasseled hat, which only rulers could wear, is like a crown in other cultures. The scepter he carries, probably made of jade, also symbolizes his authority.

Some historians say that a city that archaeologists have found near the modern city of Zhengshou was once the Xia capital. It's true that the remains of an ancient city (from around 2000 to 1500 BCE, the right time period) are in that spot, and some early writers said that this was where an important Xia city was located. However, this site could be an early city of the Shang. More cautious historians say that until somebody finds written records or other firm evidence that the Xia existed, it's safer to assume that the rulers and their culture were mythical.

The history of early China is much more complicated than myths and legends tell us. For thousands of years Chinese historians have documented their great civilization. In fact, China has the longest uninterrupted written history of any human culture. Ancient scholars collected important documents, some written as long as 3,000 years ago, into the *Book of Documents*. A fourth-century BCE book called *Tradition of Zuo* is China's first history that tries to tell a story.

History did more than record the past. Chinese rulers knew that future generations would read about them in history books and they didn't want their names to be linked with bad deeds. They must have sometimes kept this in mind when deciding how to behave in certain situations. Some rulers had a more direct method of dealing with documents that showed them in a bad light: they would execute historians who refused to change their record of a fact that wasn't flattering to the emperor. As a result, modern historians do not know if what they are reading has been influenced by a powerful ruler or if they can trust its accuracy.

Today, historians study these ancient Chinese texts and other books, and they work with archaeologists, anthropologists, **paleontologists**, and other scholars to uncover the real story of China, one of the oldest civilizations in the world. Every year scientists and scholars find out more about the great artists, thinkers, builders, warriors, and politicians and the way of life they established thousands of years ago, which still influences the lives of billions of people today.

GOD OR MAN?

A modern scholar named Gu Jiegang showed that the early Chinese thought of Yu as a god, not a human. Early documents say that Yu gave things to "this land below," which would be an odd thing to say about someone living on the land, the way people do. Yu is also said to "spread out the earth" and "array the mountains"—not the typical acts of a leader, even a wise and strong one.

The symbol used to write Yu's name: 禹 includes a part used in words for insects and reptiles (虫). Gu thinks that Yu was a lizard and suggests that he might have originally been a reptile-god that later generations saw as human.

A paleontologist is a scientist who studies the fossils of extinct animals and plants.

CHAPTER 1

PEKING MAN
EARLY HUMANS IN CHINA

❝ Miao folk song, author and date unknown

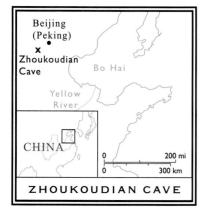

ZHOUKOUDIAN CAVE

北京
bei + jing = "north" + "capital"
Beijing is the capital of China and is in the North China Plain.

Heavenly King was intelligent,
Spat a lot of spittle into his hand,
Clapped his hands with a noise,
Produced heaven and earth,
Tall grass made insects,
Stories made men and demons,
Made men and demons,
Made male and made female.
How is it you don't know?

This folk song comes from the Miao, a minority group that has lived in China for centuries. They have migrated all over the world and call themselves the Hmong. Their song gives an interesting version of the creation of the universe and humans, but it's not one you're likely to find in a history book. Obviously, Chinese people didn't come from spit, and animals didn't just emerge from tall grass all by themselves.

Paleontologists have found that long before human beings lived in the land that we now call China, other animals roamed its mountains, wide plains, and deep valleys. It must have been a busy place during the time of the dinosaurs—scientists have found many fossils there. The ancient Chinese knew about the fossils, and, in fact, it's possible that some of the dragon legends that they have told for centuries were inspired by the dinosaur bones that farmers or builders uncovered.

Scientists and historians have always known that people have lived in China for a long, long time. But how long? And how did the earliest Chinese live?

The first part of an answer came in 1929. Archaeologists were digging in a cave called Zhoukoudian in a hilly, grassy area about 25 miles southwest of **Beijing**, the capital of modern China, when a worker found an unimportant-looking lump of bone.

"I asked [the worker] what it was," archaeologist Jia Lanpo later recalled. "He said, 'Just a piece of rotten leek.' I looked again and said, 'Get away! That's a human bone.'"

Jia Lanpo, who became one of China's greatest archaeologists, was 88 years old in 1997 when he recalled that exciting moment when speaking to a reporter. What is so memorable about a piece of bone so small and in such bad condition that it could be mistaken for a rotten vegetable? Why would Jia Lanpo, almost 70 years later, remember so vividly the moment the worker showed it to him?

The answer is that this piece of bone turned out to be special. It was part of the skullcap, or top of the skull, of an individual belonging to the species *Homo erectus*, humanlike creatures that lived in China between 200,000 and 700,000 years ago. *Homo erectus* first appeared in Africa about 1.5 million years ago, but the Zhoukoudian Cave fossils were the earliest humanlike remains found in Asia. Archaeologists eventually found the skullcaps and remains of more than 40 other examples of *Homo erectus* in Zhoukoudian Cave and named them "Peking Man" in honor of the nearby city.

The archaeologists in China weren't the only people to be excited by the find. Word spread quickly around the world. On December 16, 1929, the *New York Times* reported about the "discovery in a cave near Peking of the fossilized bones of ten men, who possibly lived 1,000,000 years ago." The journalists who first broke the story were so excited that they misinterpreted some of what the archaeologists had found; at that point they had uncovered only some teeth and a few skullcaps. Archaeologists would find more fossils later.

The reporters can be forgiven for getting some of the facts wrong. Even today it's difficult to date the remains precisely

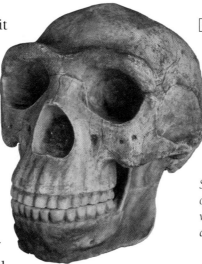

❝ Peking Man, Beijing, 400,000 years ago

Scientists can tell from the large size of Peking Man's skull that his brain was the size of an early human's, not an ape's.

WEREN'T THERE ANY PEKING WOMEN?

The *Homo erectus* ("upright human") whose remains were found in Zhoukoudian Cave are known today as "Peking Man." "Peking" is an old-fashioned spelling of "Beijing," and humans and humanlike creatures of both sexes and of all ages used to be referred to as "man." Scientists classify this species as *Homo erectus pekinensis* ("upright human of Beijing"), so a more modern way to say "Peking Man" might be "early Beijing people."

and even more difficult to figure out how Peking Man lived. Some of the questions that archaeologists and other scientists are working on include the following:

Humans are hominids. A hominid is any mammal that resembles a human being.

- Did Peking Man use fire? Most scholars say yes, based on ashes and burned bones found in some sites where these *Homo erectus* lived, but some say that Peking Man didn't really use the fires, and that they just had the bad luck to suffer through an accidental fire. Some of those who say yes think that even though these **hominids** probably weren't intelligent enough to build a fire, they might have gathered burning coals after lightning strikes and used them for light, heat, protection from wild animals, and maybe even for cooking.

- Could Peking Man talk? Their skeletons show a hole too small to allow for a larynx (voice box). On the other hand, they probably hunted large animals, including a now-extinct form of elephant. This task would surely require some kind of communication among hunters. They could pass on some knowledge of toolmaking and other skills with gestures, but speech would help.

- Should Peking Man be classified as an advanced ape or an early human? Most scientists today say human. This isn't so much a question of fact as of interpretation, because different scientists classify humans in different ways.

JAVA MAN OR JAVA APE?

A few decades before Peking Man's remains were found, anthropologists had uncovered the bones of another hominid on Java, a large island southeast of China. They originally classified the species as a large ape, *Pithecanthropus erectus,* but later determined that the remains were *Homo erectus*. Java Man was earlier than Peking Man and is considered to be more primitive.

Whether or not they had fire, could speak, or were human, hominids such as Peking Man had a hard life. The remains found in Zhoukoudian Cave show that more than half of these hominids died before age 14 and most of the rest didn't live much longer. Peking Man knew how to make some tools out of the quartz and other minerals in the area, but even so, many tasks must have taken a long time to complete. Preventing illness caused by poor diet was almost impossible, and disease and accidents must have been common. Predators such as cave bears, mountain

Evidence for fire at Zhoukoudian.

Archaeologists are still arguing about whether the dark layer in this floor cut from Zhoukoudian Cave is made of ashes from fires used by Peking Man.

lions, and hyenas attacked Peking Man, who would have found it difficult to fight them off.

Fortunately for these early humans, they lived in a time when what is now China was pretty warm. Trees and other plants supplied berries, nuts, and seeds for food. Peking Man also took advantage of the wildlife that flourished in the area. In Zhoukoudian Cave one archaeologist found the remains of more than 3,000 deer. It's unclear whether Peking Man killed these deer and other animals or scavenged them from other predators.

Over the centuries, passing carnivores gnawed on the bones in Zhoukoudian Cave, and silt and rock gradually covered them. They lay undisturbed for thousands and thousands of years until archaeologists found two hominid teeth there in 1923. That discovery led to the excavations that uncovered the rest of the remains in the next decades. The work continues and archaeologists keep finding out more details about the lives of these early humans.

Casts were made of the first fossils of Peking Man. This turned out to be fortunate for modern scientists, because some of the most important bones themselves have vanished. During World War II, the Chinese entrusted five of the precious skulls to American Marines, asking them to take them out of the country before the Japanese could seize them. Just one month later, the United States entered the war, and all U.S. servicemen in China became prisoners of war. The skulls disappeared.

Jia Lanpo, who had been present when the first skullcap was unearthed, was heartbroken. For the rest of his life, he was tormented by the loss of these precious relics of the earliest people to live in China.

After World War II ended, a new group took over China: the Communists, led by Mao Zedong. China closed itself off from much of the rest of the world as it struggled to establish its new identity. During those years of turmoil,

Visitors to Zhoukoudian Cave can see the homes of the earliest inhabitants of China. The cave seems remote, but it is actually very close to modern Beijing.

the study of China's past got pushed onto the back burner. China was too poor to invest large amounts of money in archaeology, and the government did not allow foreigners to participate in many activities in its country, including archaeological digs. Work continued as well as the Chinese scholars could manage. The Chinese government set up a national Institute of Archaeology in 1950, but in the 1960s and 1970s, the government persecuted intellectuals, including many archaeologists. Still, the scientists did make some important finds during that time.

Today archaeologists and paleontologists from around the world are working side by side with Chinese scholars, making exciting finds that shed new light on the distant past. But the loss of those precious early fossils continues to haunt archaeologists all over the world.

Shortly before Jia Lanpo's death, his son received a mysterious phone call. "A man...called me on April 2, 2001," he told reporters. "He asked me to tell my then hospitalized father that all the skulls of Peking Man lost during World War II were still in China." Wang said that another man, named Li Zhaodong, had rescued the skulls and hidden them away.

Historians are anxious to talk to Li Zhaodong, but he is in prison under investigation for corruption, and the authorities won't allow anyone to talk to him, even about such an important matter. So the mystery remains.

What happened to the early humans represented by Peking Man? Did they die out? Some scientists think so, and speculate that modern humans are descended from a different group of hominids that spread out from Africa. But other scholars, especially in China, think that Peking Man not only survived, but also flourished, and that some part of them lives on in today's Chinese people.

Of course, hominids such as Peking Man had no way of knowing they were living in China. In fact, there would be no such place as "China" for thousands of years. But many years ago people in China started establishing ways of life that would shape the great civilization to come.

IN CHINA, DOGS SAY "WANGWANG"

For Peking Man, the ancestors of the dog were feared as predators and resented as competitors for game. But by examining canine DNA, scientists have recently discovered that dogs were most likely first domesticated in East Asia shortly after Peking Man lived there, perhaps as long ago as 40,000 or even 100,000 years in the past. The Pekingese, pug, Sharpei, Shih-tzu, and Chow Chow, as well as less popular breeds such as the Chinese Crested and the Foo Dog, are ancient breeds that originated in China many years later. The Lhasa Apso comes from nearby Tibet.

CHAPTER 2

"SURPRISE AND DELIGHT"

THE DISCOVERY OF CHINA'S FIRST CULTURE

An artifact is anything made by humans. Archaeologists use "artifact" to refer to physical remains of human activity.

Longshan pots, North China, 5000–3000 BCE

These pots had been underground for thousands of years when archaeologist J. G. Andersson found them in the 1920s. Because they were buried, the colors of their beautiful swirling patterns remained fresh and undamaged by air and moisture.

One day in 1920 a man named Liu Changshan showed a collection of **artifacts** to a Swedish archaeologist and paleontologist named Johan Gunnar Andersson. Liu said that he had found them in a site near a town then called Yang Shao Tsun in English (its modern name is Yangshao). "Imagine my surprise and delight," Andersson later wrote in his book, *Children of the Yellow Earth*, when he saw in Liu's collection

> several hundred axes, knives and other objects of stone, many of them exceptionally fine and well-preserved. The collection was all the more remarkable as Liu related that he had purchased everything from the inhabitants of a single village, Yang Shao Tsun, where the peasants had collected the coveted objects in their fields.

Soon Andersson and other archaeologists unearthed more remains of a culture that has become known as "Yangshao." Today archaeologists no longer consider that town to be a good representative of pure Yangshao culture, as other societies intermingled there. Instead, today's historians look at four different sites in the river valleys of the North China plain to find out what life was like there between 7,000 and 5,000 years ago (5000 to 3000 BCE).

Andersson and later researchers found that this time was an important turning point in the history of the Chinese people, the time when their ancestors first settled down and began to build permanent settlements. Although the life of a wandering tribe has advantages, the Yangshao people were among the first to discover the benefits of staying put.

HONGSHAN
North China Plain
Bo Hai
Shandong Peninsula
Yellow Sea
Yellow River
YANGSHAO
Banpo · · Jiangzhai
Yangzi River
HEMUDU
Hangzhou Bay
East China Sea

CHINA'S FIRST CULTURES, 5000 BCE

0   400 mi
0   600 km

The first benefit of settling down is that it's easier to keep an eye on your food supply. Today the North China plain is dry, with thick layers of yellow soil. But at the time of the Yangshao people, forests filled with wild game covered the land. Among the tools that archaeologists have found in the villages are arrowheads and spear points made of both stone and bone. They have also uncovered bones of the animals that the Yangshao people hunted with their arrows and spears: small animals such as rats, raccoons, rabbits, and foxes, and also wild boar, deer, leopards, and rhinoceros.

But wild game wasn't their only source of meat. The sites show remains of domestic dogs and pigs in almost all Yangshao-era villages, and evidence of sheep, goats, and cattle has turned up in some areas. Nomadic people sometimes keep livestock, but it's hard to herd semiwild animals while on the move. It's much easier to keep them penned up or at least to get them accustomed to coming to one place every day for food so that you can keep track of them. So one major benefit to a settled abode is having a more reliable source of meat. A drawback is that sometimes you have to bring food to the animals, since once they are confined to one area they can't wander to new pastures after they've eaten everything in a field or after the growing period ends in your area.

The Yangshao people mostly settled along rivers, a good source of food both then and now. Wandering people could move to where the fish were running in a given season, which certainly is an advantage. However, by staying in one place, the people could learn the natural rhythms of the particular fish in their area, and would be right on the spot when the fish were passing by. The people would learn the best places to catch different fish and could return to them at times that had been good in the past. The Yangshao people made hooks, harpoons, and nets to catch fish.

Rivers bring not only fish, but better crops. The people built their houses on terraces near the Yellow River, which gets its name from the mud churned up by its swiftly flowing water. During floods and high water the river deposits the mud along the banks, where it becomes fertile farmland.

Early humans often moved around, following crops as they ripened. But the

This pot, with its ghostly childlike face, was probably used in some type of ritual. The spout is located in the back, so that when a person poured from the vessel, he could see this little face staring at him through its half-opened eyes.

more settled Yangshao people, while they certainly continued to pick edible plants as they found them, also came up with something else, a development that changed their lives and the lives of their descendants: farming.

By studying the fields where the Yangshao people farmed, archaeologists have figured out that workers prepared the fields for the crops by cutting down trees and burning off the grasses and weeds. The ash from the fires fertilized the soil, but even so, after a while the repeated harvests of the same crop would use up nutrients and the farmers would have to abandon the field. Then the cycle would start all over again in a fresh area. The farmers' main crop was a grain called **millet**. Archaeologists have unearthed planting implements and some grindstones that the Yangshao people used to turn some of the millet they harvested into flour.

Meanwhile, outside the Yangshao area, another group, called the Hemudu people, had started cultivating rice, a crop that has been associated with Asia ever since. Rice needs a lot of water to grow, and the Hemudu people lived near marshes on the southern side of Hangzhou Bay. Archaeologists have found huge amounts of the inedible parts of the rice plant in Hemudu garbage heaps. Like the Yangshao, the Hemudu culture had domestic dogs and pigs, and the people hunted.

People who plant seeds, tend young plants, fertilize soil, and harvest a crop months later have to stay settled. They also have to be able to plan for the future in a different way from people who move from place to place, taking advantage of migrations of animals and planting seasons in different areas. This doesn't mean that nonfarmers aren't as intelligent as farmers, but it does mean that the two groups think of the future in different ways.

If you have to stick around, you might as well be comfortable, so the farming people built sturdy houses. To survive, they had to band together with others to fight off predators and to help in the work. So these people built their houses near each other. Their small villages probably had land in common, not private property, and all the inhabitants shared in the hard work of growing crops and taking care of animals.

Millet is an important grain in Africa and Asia. Millet flour can't be used to make bread in raised loaves. Instead it is usually eaten in a flat bread (like a cracker) or as a porridge.

TEMPLE BUILDERS

Another culture of about the same time period as the Yangshao and the Hemudu is the Hongshan, in the northeast of modern China. Archaeologists have unearthed the foundations of large religious complexes, which are the earliest religious buildings found in China. Perhaps the mother goddess whose statues have also been excavated at Hongshan was worshipped there. The Hongshan people also carved a hard-to-work stone, jade, into small figures.

The Yangshao village now called Banpo is typical of the kind of settlement that these early people built. The village is laid out in a rough oval with the houses and storage areas in the center, surrounded by a large moat that was 16 to 20 feet (5 to 6 meters) deep and wide and perhaps served as a defense against other people and wild animals. Archaeologists have excavated 46 houses at Banpo in the 30,000-square meter area surrounded by the moat. The houses were small by today's standards—10 to 16 feet (3 to 5 meters) across—and were constructed partially below ground level. The walls were made of a type of construction called "wattle and daub," in which mud is plastered to wooden supports. Later Yangshao people learned how to build fires near the walls to bake them as hard as modern bricks.

The houses at Banpo faced the central square. On the east were the kilns (ovens for firing, or baking, clay). The Yangshao people made bowls, basins, and jars of different shapes and sizes. This is another advantage of staying in one place: people who wander around can't use a large and immovable construction like a kiln.

The objects made in the kilns weren't just useful. The skilled potters also made them beautiful, decorating them

❝ Banpo village, Shaanxi, about 4000 BCE

Archaeologists preserved the excavated Banpo village of about 4000 BCE in its original spot, making the whole site a museum. The outlines of the houses still remain in the ground.

by pressing twisted cords or woven mats onto the clay to create designs. Artists painted some of the pieces with geometric designs, animals, or odd faces.

Archaeologists working at Banpo were excited to find pots with marks near the rim. These marks, which had been cut into the wet clay before firing, may identify either the pot's maker or its owner. Some people think that these marks are the ancestors of Chinese writing, but most scholars think similarities between the designs in the pottery and writing are accidental. Still, the marks are evidence that the people of Banpo understood the concept of representing an idea with a mark, the basis for a written language.

Archaeologists have found some of the best quality pots, as well as ornaments and tools, in graves. For this reason, historians assume that the Yangshao people believed in an afterlife, and that these objects were left for the person to use in the next world.

When someone from a group of wandering people dies, the body obviously must be left behind. In a more settled culture, people can visit graves and perhaps begin to think of their dead relatives in a different way. The cemetery at Banpo is located outside the settlement's living area, and contains the bodies of 130 adults. The corpses are stretched out as though sleeping faceup, with their heads all pointing to the west. There could very well be some religious significance in the fact that they are laid out as though they were going in the direction of the setting sun.

The Yangshao people treated the bodies of infants and young children differently from those of adults. They were buried in urns (large pots), often with a hole on the top. Nobody knows why young people weren't buried in the same way as the adults, and what is the meaning of the hole in their burial urns. Some scholars think that this might be a way to allow their souls to escape.

The faces decorating this bowl are a combination of masks and fish. They might represent different Banpo families, or they might depict spirits that villagers prayed to when using the bowl.

Bowl, Banpo, about 4000 BCE

MEANWHILE IN THE AMERICAS...

The Chinchorro people, who lived in what are now Chile and Peru, carefully preserved their dead, starting about 5000 to 3000 BCE. They took the bodies apart, dried and preserved them with chemicals, and reassembled them. They then painted the skin, often with many layers, leading some scholars to think that the bodies were displayed or used in religious ceremonies, so the paint was reapplied as it wore away.

The graves also give clues about the society of the Yangshao people. Archaeologists usually find more and better grave goods (objects buried with the corpse) with the bodies of some people than with others and assume that these people were more important or more powerful than others. But in Yangshao graveyards, most of the graves have few grave goods, which makes scholars think that most people were equal in the society—most, but not all. Archaeologists would often find just one tomb with especially rich grave goods. They think that this may have been the grave of the chief. For example, one Yangshao grave in the village of Jiangzhai, near Xian, had 8,577 bone beads, 12

The peaked roofs made of thatch (bundles of grasses) on houses from Banpo village allowed rain to run off. The villagers dug most of their houses into the ground a few feet, which kept the houses cooler in the summer and protected them from cold wind in the winter.

Why were all these Yangshao people buried together? Did they die in an epidemic? Were they killed together in battle or by a natural disaster? Nobody knows. One fact that is pretty sure is that they were important in their society, as they were buried with expensive painted pots.

Why were all these Yangshao people buried together? Did they die in an epidemic? Were they killed together in battle or by a natural disaster? Nobody knows. One fact that is pretty sure is that they were important in their society, as they were buried with expensive painted pots.

stone beads, and a number of red pottery vessels, while the other graves held very few artifacts.

The Yangshao people lived in the area that was to become central to Chinese history. Many of the most important aspects of later Chinese civilization existed in an early form here and among other people, such as those of the Hemudu culture. The small villages would eventually become powerful cities. The symbolic marks in hard-baked clay eventually were replaced by a complex writing system that made it possible for the members of a complex society to govern themselves and to express themselves in beautiful literature. Skilled craftspeople improved the quality and speed of production of handcrafts such as pottery. These improvements made their objects more important not only in daily life but also as export items that helped support the growing society. The love of decoration and the skill of artists shown on the decorated pottery grew until the Chinese were creating wonderful works of art. Domestic animals and crops, such as millet and rice, played a central role in feeding what was to become a huge civilization. Religion and worship of ancestors became the focus of much of life. Many of these characteristics would never have developed in a wandering people.

But it was another group that provided some of the basic principles and structures that began to define ancient China. These people are known today as the Longshan.

YOUNG SPIRITS

In cultures where many people die young, it's sometimes customary for children not to be considered part of the community, or even fully human, until they've reached a certain age. Perhaps the babies of the Yangshao culture were buried near their homes in the hopes that their spirits would get a second chance at life with that family.

CHAPTER 3

LONGSHAN
CHINA'S FIRST CIVILIZATION

To find the first real civilization in China—the first to set up large cities, to organize big groups of people for large-scale building projects, and to divide their population into social groups—you have to move east to the Shandong peninsula where the people now called "Longshan" lived, probably from about 3000 to 2000 BCE.

In 1928 archaeologists found remains of the Longshan civilization near the modern city of Chengziyai. They were startled at the size of a wall they found: about 20 feet (6 meters) high and 30 feet (9 meters) wide at the top. These archaeologists recognized the method used to construct the

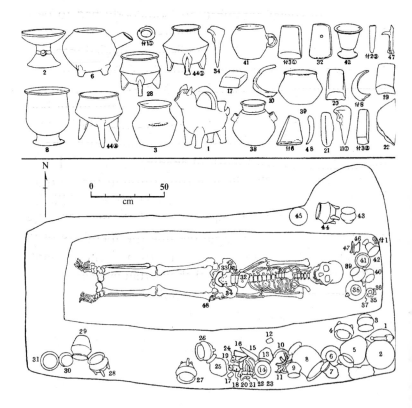

The number and quality of objects displayed in this drawing of a Longshan tomb show that the person buried there was important and wealthy. Archaeologists carefully draw what they uncover. The position of artifacts often gives them clues about the culture that they are investigating.

wall, called stamped earth. When they carefully separated the hard layers of dirt, they found round marks each the size of the end of a log. The method of packing down earth with logs until it is solid is a typical Chinese building method that would be used for thousands of years to make walls and roads.

The wall not only proved that the Longshan people were good at construction, but it also meant that they had something to defend. The most common reason to erect a barrier between you and the rest of the world is to keep out enemies who might kill you or take your possessions—or both. Other finds at Chengziyai show that the Longshan people were guarding themselves from enemies. Of 116 stone implements found in Chengziyai, 28 were weapons, mainly spearheads and arrowheads. Weapons made up an even larger proportion (29 out of 53) of bone tools. The large number of weapons and the large wall must mean that the Longshan people were often at war.

In order to build such a big wall, the Longshan needed some kind of social organization. Somebody had to be in charge of the project, and the laborers needed to know what work to do. This meant that people were divided into classes. Most ancient civilizations in China were sharply divided along class lines, and even their tales show how different they thought well-born and lower-born people were. One creation legend says that the goddess Nüwa made the first humans out of yellow mud. She got tired of doing the hard work of shaping them and decided to take a shortcut. She drew a rope through the mud and flicked it, producing misshapen globs. She breathed life into any pieces of mud that looked reasonably human. The first, more carefully crafted people became the members of the upper class, whereas the cruder ones turned into peasants.

The cemetery at Chengziyai shows that even after death, class distinctions continued. Scholars have divided the graves into four groups, based on the number and quality of

Eggshell-thin pottery was too fragile for everyday use. Long-stemmed goblets such as this one from the Longshan culture were probably used in religious ceremonies, perhaps in drinking a toast to the dead.

[66] Pottery cup, Longshan culture, 2500–2000 BCE

CUTTING WITH DUST

A diamond is one of the hardest materials occurring in nature. Today diamond cutters often use human-made materials to cut the stones, but in earlier days they used diamond dust in much the same way that the Longshan used sand on jade.

Something abrasive is scratchy, able to wear something away. }

Bronze is an alloy (mixture) of copper and some other metal, usually tin. }

🔊 Jade axe, Longshan culture, 2500–2000 BCE

This jade axe blade was never intended for practical use. Instead, when it was attached to a handle (now lost), it would have been used in a ritual ceremony of some kind.

the grave goods found in them. Five graves out of the 87 found there look like they belong to the members of the highest class: the graves are large, with a ledge to hold some of the objects, such as finely crafted cups, buried with the corpse. Fifty-four are narrow, with no grave goods at all. The others fall somewhere in between. It's likely that when they were alive, only a small proportion of people was on top whereas most were at lower levels of society.

The Longshan people made very fine pottery, sometimes using a wheel, which makes more symmetrical and attractive pots than the coiled-rope method that the earlier Yangshao people had adopted. Some of this pottery was as thin as an eggshell, and when fired (baked at high temperatures), it became extremely hard. The skilled craftspeople also carved jade, a highly prized green stone, into different shapes.

Jade is very difficult to work, requiring not only talent but also good tools and training. In fact, jade is harder than any of the tools that people of the time could make. So how did they cut it? Someone long ago noticed that sand was very **abrasive** and figured out that by rubbing the same spot on a piece of jade over and over again with grit, you could eventually wear a hole or a line. Skilled craftspeople would dip a string in wet sand and rub it on the jade until the string broke, and then repeat the action over and over again with more pieces of string until the shape emerged.

The ancient artisans continued to develop and refine their pottery-making and jade-working techniques. Much later they transferred their skills to other areas, such as **bronze** casting and lacquer work.

What makes the Longshan people especially interesting is that modern people can see how important ritual was in

their lives. Rituals today can vary from something like a family tradition—always celebrating the first warm day of spring with a picnic, for example, or making a certain cake on someone's birthday—to more serious customs such as celebrations of religious holidays with a traditional meal or special prayers. Modern Chinese people find rituals very important, and it appears that their long-ago ancestors did too. The long-stemmed drinking cups found in some tombs probably had a religious use, since archaeologists discovered them in graves of people from the upper classes and their shapes are different from the small cups used every day. Carved jade found in graves shows that surviving family members and friends thought it was important for the dead person to have precious and beautiful objects in the next life. Some of the jade was worked into the shapes of animals or demons, meaning that the Longshan culture probably had some kind of mythology.

At Chengziyai archaeologists have also found shoulder bones of deer that had been placed in a fire until they cracked. This might not seem very exciting, but historians see this as a definite link between the people of Chengziyai and the Shang, the first dynasty that everyone agrees existed. The Shang believed that they could read the cracks in shoulder bones of large animals to predict the future and to find out what the gods and spirits wanted. When modern Chinese people found these shoulder bones in about 1900, they didn't know what they were, and thought they must have come from dragons.

Perhaps the people who found these bones would have been even more intrigued if they had known that far from coming from dragons, the bones were really religious items made by their distant ancestors. But it wasn't until later in the 20th century that archaeologists, historians, and other scholars put together the clues to unravel the mystery of the "dragon bones" and the odd-looking cracks that were supposed to reveal the will of the gods.

LUCKY DRAGONS

Dragons are good-luck symbols in China, not the scary creatures of European legend. Chinese dragons live in the water, so they can't breathe fire, but they can fly. They cause floods when they race down a river. When they play in the clouds, they cause rain, so farmers pray to them during dry spells. A Chinese dragon has a camel's head, a demon's eyes, a cow's ears, a deer's antlers, a snake's neck, a clam's belly (do clams have bellies?), a tiger's paws, and an eagle's claws. It is covered with 117 scales like those on a large fish called a carp.

Most Chinese dragons are shown with four claws. A five-clawed dragon represents the emperor, and anyone else showing a five-clawed dragon on clothes, art, or decoration would be put to death.

CHAPTER 4

EVERYBODY TALKS ABOUT THE WEATHER
AGRICULTURE AND ORACLES

If rain doesn't fall at the right time, or if a frost kills the crop, people starve. It would be very helpful if we could predict the weather more accurately, and even better if we could change it. Even today with the help of satellites and radar, weather forecasting is difficult and not always on target, so imagine how bewildering the whole process must have seemed thousands of years ago.

People during the rule of the Shang dynasty (about 1500 to 1046 BCE) assumed that nature gods were in charge of the weather. If only people could communicate with these gods, they could find out what they wanted and give it to them. Then, if the gods were pleased with their gifts, they might end a drought or make the air warm for growing plants.

wanted to please the gods

Scholars have sometimes found important clues to humanity's past in China's drugstores. The German pale-ontologist who purchased "dragon teeth" 100 years ago was interested in human prehistory, not in grinding these fossils into medicine.

The problem is that you can't call up a god and ask for a favor. People in most ancient cultures thought that they could at least take a guess about the gods' will by observing natural events—storms, animal behavior, cloud formations, and so forth. But it turns out that the people of the Shang era also used another form of communication, one that was forgotten for a long, long time and rediscovered only by chance.

In 1899, almost 3000 years after the end of the Shang dynasty, a sick man named Wang Yirong said that his doctor had prescribed for his illness ground-up "dragon bones"—fossils and relics that most Chinese people at the time thought came from long-dead dragons. His family brought him belly-shells of turtles from the pharmacy. Wang, a scholar who could read ancient Chinese writing, realized that what looked like scratches on the shells were actually words. He told his family not to grind them up, and began looking for other shells and bones.

People who collected "dragon bones" for medicine found many of them in a village called Xiaotun near Anyang in Henan Province, on the banks of the twisting Huan River. As Wang Yirong's news spread, scholars from China, the United States, and Japan began visiting this dry area, digging in the yellow, windblown dust to unearth the mysterious bones. Chinese archaeologists began formal excavations in 1928. The inscriptions on these bones show the most ancient Chinese writing that has survived to modern times.

Why would people write on bones? Didn't they have anything else to use? Well, yes, but these flat, thin bones were special. For some unknown reason, the ancient Chinese people thought that turtle shells and shoulder bones of oxen had a special connection to the world of the gods. If people handled the "dragon bones" correctly, they thought, they could use them as a kind of instant messenger to the heavens.

Correct handling involved a special ceremony where the king asked a question. A priest drilled two shallow pots into the bone or shell.

The priest then pressed a hot metal bar into the bone until the heat made it crack. The BOK sound that the bone made when it cracked opposite the holes sounded similar to the

The first step in preparing an oracle bone was to bore pits into the back. Touching a hot rod to these pits made the cracks on the other side.

🔊 Oracle bone, 1500–1000 BCE

MEANWHILE IN CRETE...

At about the same time that people in China were developing their writing, people on the island of Crete, in what is now Greece, were doing the same. They used symbols in two different systems of writing that are now called "Linear A" and "Linear B." Nobody today can read Linear A, but a scholar named Michael Ventris deciphered Linear B in 1952. It turned out to be an early form of Greek.

❝ Oracle bone, Anyang, 1200–1080 BCE

Sometimes it was hard to get a straight answer out of the gods. To cover all bases, Shang diviners often asked the gods the same question many times, sometimes in both positive and negative forms ("Will it rain? Will it not rain?"). On this oracle bone, from about 1200 BCE, diviners wrote positive questions and their answers on the right, and negative questions and their answers on the left.

ancient word for "divination" (foretelling the future), which is now pronounced *bu.*

The priest would interpret the pattern made by the cracks—nobody knows how he did this—to find the answer to the question. Someone, a priest, the king, or someone else, would then write the gods' answer on the bone.

People must have been very anxious to find out what the gods had said. Everything—not just weather, but the king's health, the outcome of wars, luck in a hunt—depended on the gods' protection. If the gods and spirits were in a good mood, they might give people information that would help them with their lives. They would tell them what to do to cure an illness, or give advice about whether rain would ruin a hunting party, or let them know if the queen was going to have a boy or a girl.

The gods and dead ancestors (parents, grandparents, great-grandparents, and so on, who were also a kind of god) would speak through the bones to tell people what would keep them happy. The king might ask: "Should we send someone to the river to throw in three sheep and sacrifice three oxen?" Sometimes it might be hard to figure out which spirit was angry. The answer to a question such as "Is it Ancestral Father Ding who is cursing the king?" would narrow down the field to the ancestor whose feelings needed to be soothed.

The Shang believed that sacrifices kept the touchy gods and equally touchy ancestors happy. Because many animals would be slaughtered, the rituals that the king performed were very expensive. Of course, the killing had to be done correctly. One dragon-bone inscription from the Shang period shows the king's eagerness to get the offering just right, as he asked, "Should the king pray for a good harvest to Wanghai [an early king] by offering a dog, a sheep, a pig, a burnt offering of three sets of sheep and pig, and the slaughtering of nine oxen, three piglets, and three Qiang tribesmen?"

Not only did sacrifices have to be done correctly, they also had to be performed at the right time on the right day. The calendar was so complicated that often scholars had to be consulted to resolve questions about it. The Shang scholars knew a lot about the stars and the planets. They calculated the length of a month to a very accurate 29.5 days and a solar year to 365.5 days. Inscriptions on bones speak of both solar and lunar eclipses. The Shang also observed and recorded comets and other phenomena in the night sky.

The oldest male member of every **clan** was responsible for sacrificing to his own ancestors. Although younger male members of any family could also sacrifice to their ancestors, their offerings must have been much less extravagant. The king's sacrifices would have used up so many resources that if others had such huge rituals, the country would have run out of sacrificial animals.

Like the spirits of ancestors, the gods in charge of the all-important weather weren't necessarily kind or cruel— they were more or less neutral, and how they acted toward humans depended on how the people treated them. So the king sacrificed to them as he asked questions inscribed on **oracle** bones such as, "Will the Yellow River not order it to rain?" (Like all rivers, the Yellow River was a god—probably a dragon—and river gods were responsible for rainfall.)

When a hoped-for weather outcome didn't happen, the Shang would assume that a sacrifice hadn't been done correctly or hadn't been sumptuous enough, or that there was some other reason that the nature gods didn't come through. So although the Shang kings continued to try to cajole the gods into helping out, and were cheered up when it appeared that they had responded, they had to rely on the hard work and skill of the farmers to make sure that there was enough to eat.

The king was the symbolic leader of the farmers and he performed the ritual first planting of the season. An inscription on an oracle bone asks, "Should the king lead the many

A clan is a group of people who claim descent from a common ancestor. A clan can be as small as an extended family or as large as a tribe.

An oracle is a person or object that transmits a god's communication, usually about the future.

people in planting grain?" "Should we pray for a good harvest to Di [the high god]?" asks another questioner, who wants to be sure his prayers go to the right god, and another, nervous about the fate of the crops, asks, "When we reach the fourth month, will Di make it rain?" Apparently at some point it was so dry that extra sacrifices had to be made: "If we burn a woman [as a sacrifice], will there be rain?" Not just farming, but hunting too was an important source of food and just as dependent on the gods' good will. "If we go hunting at Ji, going and coming will there be no disaster?" is one anxious question on a bone.

The largest and least powerful group in Shang-era society was made up of peasants, who worked the land and acted as servants, and craftsmen, who made the products that both the rich and the poor used. Oracles bones, the only written source from this time, seldom mention workers, and very little is known about their lives. Judging from what scholars know about other similar societies, it's probable that members of this lowest group had few rights and

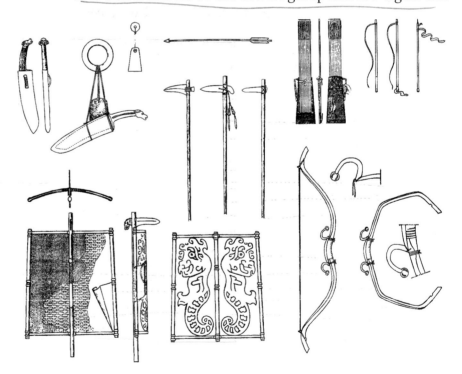

A wealthy Shang warrior would have been buried with a wide variety of weapons. Soldiers did not yet use long swords for hand-to-hand combat. Instead they preferred the wicked-looking dagger axes in the center of the drawing. Only a strong warrior could have used the double-curved bow on the right. It would have taken a great deal of strength to bend the bow enough to string it.

that their freedom was very limited. Some modern historians have described the Shang as a slave society, but there is no word for "slave" on any oracle bones, and so nobody knows whether slavery was practiced at this time.

Many people formed this lowest group, and most of them worked very hard. One early Shang city was surrounded by a wall four miles long, 60 feet thick, and 30 feet high. No records survive to say how long it took to build the wall, or how many people worked on it, but one estimate is that the total amount of labor was about 200,000 **man-years**. Then, of course, many people were required to build the palaces and everything else inside the wall. Farmers and soldiers also worked hard to keep the growing population fed and defended from enemies.

{ A man-year is a unit expressing how much work one man can do in one year. A job requiring 200,000 man-years would take 200 men 1,000 years to complete, or 2,000 men 100 years.

Although the Shang were protected by these huge walls, they always had to be on their guard against other states, and it was important to make sure that the gods were in the mood to help out when they went to war. "This season," reads a question on one oracle bone, "if the king should follow Wang Cheng to attack the Xia Wei, will we receive assistance in this case?"

Archaeologists keep turning up evidence about this long-ago time, and what they find sometimes seems grim to modern people. At a site that they think was a major city from the time of the Shang, archaeologists have found evidence of mass human sacrifice. They estimate that as many as 13,000 people lost their lives in the last 250 years of the dynasty's rule, killed to satisfy the seemingly never-ending hunger of the emperors' ancestors.

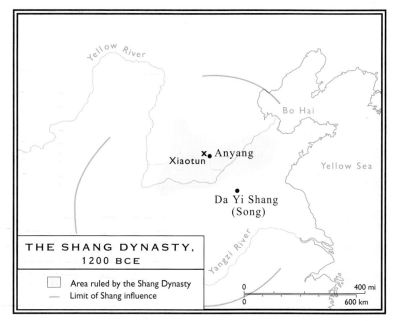

THE SHANG DYNASTY,
1200 BCE

☐ Area ruled by the Shang Dynasty
— Limit of Shang influence

0   400 mi
0   600 km

WRITING CHINESE

Unlike an alphabet in which each letter represents a sound, or a syllabary in which each character represents a syllable, usually a consonant-vowel combination, each Chinese character stands for an entire word. People in different parts of China, speaking different types of Chinese, might pronounce the same character differently, but it would have the same meaning for each of them.

Some characters are pictographs, or pictures, of the word they represent. In many cases the picture has changed so much over the centuries since it was first written that it's hard to see the resemblance. In this table, modern characters are listed below their ancient Shang versions. You can see the similarity between the modern Chinese and the ancient Shang version of the character for goat, but the ancient form is more goatlike and shows the animal's horns.

Ox	Goat, sheep	Tree	Moon	Earth	Water	Tripot vessel (ring)	To show, declare	Field	Then
屮	𢒸	朿	)	𡈼	巛	鼎	丌	田	就
牛	羊	木	月	土	水	鼎	示	田	就

Other characters are called ideographs, because they represent an idea, not a thing. The modern character meaning *good* or *to like* (好) is a combination of two characters, one meaning *woman* (女) and the other *child* (子).

For numbers, the Chinese started with horizontal lines: 一 (one), 二 (two), and 三 (three). After three, the lines became hard to count, so they found an ingenious solution for the higher numbers. For example, the word *four* and the word *neigh* were both *si*, pronounced "szz." To write four, the Chinese used the character for *neigh*, a drawing of a horse's open mouth: 㕯. The modern version looks like 四 .

Most Chinese characters are made up of one part that tells you the sound of the word and another part that gives a clue to its meaning. For example, the words for *goat* and *ocean* are both pronounced "yang." Ocean (洋) is written in two separate parts: 羊 (goat), and three dots representing drops of water 氵 . The three dots tell the reader that in this case the kind of *yang* he or she is reading about is the ocean, not the goat. More than 80 percent of Chinese characters are made up of two different parts like this.

CHAPTER 5

DRAGON BONES AND HIDDEN TREASURES

THE SHANG COURT

In 1976, archaeologists working in the royal cemetery near Anyang in central North China uncovered the tomb of Lady Hao, one of the wives of King Wuding, a powerful king of the Shang dynasty. Lady Hao, who died about 1200 BCE, was buried with a priceless collection of objects, including 7,000 cowry shells, 200 bronze vessels, 23 bronze bells, 44 bronze tools (mostly knives), over 130 weapons, 4 bronze tigers, 590 jade objects, more than 100 jade and opal beads, 70 stone sculptures and stone objects, 490 bone hairpins, and even more. The best stroke of luck for the archaeologists was that the grave had not been looted by robbers looking for treasure.

66 Ivory cup, Anyang, about 1200 BCE

This cup from Lady Hao's tomb is made of ivory from an elephant's tusk and inlaid with turquoise. In ancient times elephants lived in China's Yellow River valley, which is now too cold and dry for them.

Just the existence of these objects in the tomb tells historians two important facts about the powerful nobles of the Shang dynasty: they were enormously wealthy, and they believed that their possessions would be useful after death. When historians study the finds more closely, they learn even more about Lady Hao and her society. For example, they have learned more about how war was waged in ancient China.

Scholars gained some insight into warfare, including the surprising role that women might have sometimes played in battles. Some people might assume that women in that society were not warriors, but archaeologists found knives and other weapons in Lady Hao's tomb. Her weapons were not just ornaments, but were usable, and one inscription says that Lady Hao led the members of the Zi clan into battle.

ARCHAEOLOGY IN THE STARS

Nobody is sure why these rulers called themselves "Shang," since their family name was Zi. It's also not exactly clear what years they were in power, but it was probably around 1500 BCE to 1046 BCE. How have historians figured out the end-date so precisely? They knew from other sources that the Shang rule came to the end sometime in the mid-eleventh century BCE, but the science of archaeo-astronomy helped them pinpoint it more exactly.

Since the earth's position in relation to the stars and planets changes, people's view of the night sky has gradually shifted in the more than 3,000 years since the Shang rule came to an end. According to the *Bamboo Annals* of the third century BCE, when the Shang fell, five planets formed a regular five-sided shape in the sky: "Five stars assembled in the constellation Fang (House)." Astronomers have figured out from this information that the change from the Shang dynasty to the next family of rulers (the Zhou) took place in 1046.

Nobody likes to lose a battle, but in ancient China losing a fight could mean losing your life—another fact that Lady Hao's tomb has confirmed. Of the 16 people buried with her, some were her servants who were killed so that they could continue to wait on her in the afterlife. But many inscriptions speak of beheading war captives, so it appears that others were sacrifices, probably prisoners of war offered to the gods as a gift. Most war captives were men from the upper classes in their home states. However, when they were taken prisoner, not only did they lose their high social standing and all their rights, but some also lost their lives when they were used as human sacrifices.

Women of high rank like Lady Hao very rarely participated in battles, but it was even more unusual for women to run a state in ancient China. In most modern societies, the leader of the government is a political figure who makes policies and runs the country in peace and in war. But this isn't always been the case. In ancient China, as in many other societies, the king was mostly a military leader. If he didn't prove his skill and bravery by leading his soldiers into war, people's confidence in him would drop. The king would soon lose the support of his allies and even his own subjects, and someone else might take over. So instead of staying outside of dangerous conflicts, the king had to be directly involved, often even leading the charge against the enemy. This was risky, and sometimes the king was killed.

The men fighting alongside the king were members of the nobility, people related to the king but not in his immediate family. Only the wealthy could afford chariots and expensive bronze weapons. It takes more than one person to drive a chariot, as the driver is too busy controlling the horses to fight actively. In addition to the driver, an archer and a soldier carrying a long lance manned each chariot. Men fighting on foot used a dagger-axe and a dagger or short sword.

The rulers of other states allied with the Shang also had close ties with the king. Many of these rulers were related to the Zi clan (the Shang's extended family). Sometimes it was hard to tell which of these rulers were friends and

*It took dozens of archae-
ologists working together
to excavate the tomb of
Lady Hao. Little did they
know they would eventu-
ally reveal to the world
the long-hidden remains
of China's first female
military commander.*

which were enemies, as loyalties could shift quickly. To stay
in the king's favor, these rulers would send him gifts.
Nobody knows much about these gifts, although some oracle
bones mention special presents such as turtle shells, and
written sources from the next dynasty mention that the
Shang received this kind of tribute. It's likely that some of
the treasures in Lady Hao's tomb were presents given to her
or her husband. In return, the king sometimes used his connection with his powerful royal ancestors to ask them questions and seek their blessing for his followers and allies. He
also offered military advice and assistance when states that
were loyal to him were in danger.

Below the nobility came other men who had a little less
power, and who were probably distant relatives of the king.
They were sometimes the younger sons of local chiefs.
Family ties were an important source of the king's power,
since only direct descendants (sons, grandsons, great
grandsons, and so on) of earlier rulers could sacrifice to the
spirits of the ancestors.

It was hard, perhaps impossible, for people to shift position in Shang society. The anonymous farmers, workers,

IT DEPENDS ON WHAT YOU CALL "LUCKY"

One oracle bone gives the
king's interpretation of the
cracks that were made on
the bone. The question
inscribed on the bone was
"When Lady Hao [the king's
wife] gives birth to a child,
will it be lucky?" Later, the
comment "It was not lucky,
it was a girl" was inscribed
on the same bone.

A warrior buried with horses and a chariot would be prepared to carry on his life as a soldier in the world of the dead.

FAITHFUL FOLLOWERS

Often, archaeologists find more than one body in the tomb of an important person. Sometimes the bodies were those of war captives who were beheaded and left under the coffin as sacrifices to the earth, and sometimes they were those of servants.

Most of these servants were probably minor nobles who felt it was an honor to work closely with the important person. They might have felt that it was also an honor to accompany their master or mistress to the other world. Perhaps they thought that life in the other world was bound to be better than life in this one, and they were eager to go there. In any case, some of them were buried alive, along with the weapons or tools that they needed to carry on their work. It appears that most (if not all) of them went to their deaths willingly. Modern scholars call this custom "following in death."

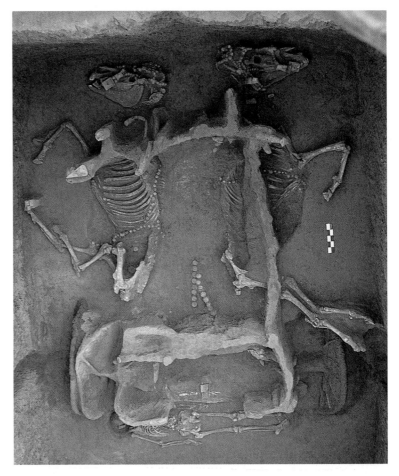

and laborers at the bottom made up the largest group. They had no education and no way of moving up in life. The king also had no choice in his occupation—although he probably didn't see this as a bad thing. He was always the oldest living son in the main line of the ruling family. This meant that when he died, the throne did not automatically pass to his own son, but to his next-oldest brother, if he had one. When there were no brothers left, the oldest son of the oldest brother became the next king. Although only men could be king, royal women such as Lady Hao possessed both wealth and power. Many historians, looking at her rich grave goods and knowing that she sometimes led troops into battle, think that royal women had more power in the Shang dynasty than women have held in China at other times.

Archaeologists have been searching in different parts of the area that the Shang controlled, trying to find out more evidence about their lives. They are starting to put together the evidence they have uncovered to figure out what life was like. One thing that is clear is that craftspeople flourished. Fortunately for modern archaeologists, one of the crafts at which the Shang were expert was bronze working. Bronze is durable—as long as nobody melts it down—so many bronze objects from the Shang dynasty have survived in tombs such as that of Lady Hao. Expert artisans made weapons, armor, pots, stoves, musical instruments, and many other items from this metal. The ability to work bronze into objects was so important that modern historians call the whole time period of 1500 to 400 BCE in China the Bronze Age.

In the second millennium BCE Chinese bronze workers developed a bronze-production method (the "piece-mold process") that enabled them to make hollow pieces such as pots and urns. First, a craftsman made a clay model of the finished product. Once the model dried, a worker pressed wet clay around it, and when the clay had dried, he carefully removed the outer layer in sections, preserving the shape of the model on its inside surface. These pieces were baked until hard and then reassembled into a mold. Then a very skillful and very careful craftsman poured in the hot liquid bronze. When it cooled, the finished piece could be removed from the mold. The same model could be used over and over again.

Historians have also relied on written accounts as well as artifacts such as bronze vessels for details about the Shang dynasty. The writings say that although the first Shang king was a good ruler,

The artist who created this wine vessel more than 3,000 years ago was more interested in decoration than in showing a realistic elephant.

The grinning demon on this axe blade might have been the last thing some people would see. The axe was used for beheading sacrificial victims.

not all of the kings who came after him governed wisely. The last king of the dynasty, Di Xin, was especially bad. For one thing, according to Sima Qian's "Basic Annals" of about 100 BCE, he supposedly killed his uncle by having his heart cut out while he was alive. The author of this account says that instead of spending his time governing his people, that king "made a lake filled with wine and hung slabs of meat to make a forest, and then had men and women chase each other through the forest, partying all night long."

The problem with relying on these descriptions of Shang court life is that they were written by people working for the next rulers, who wanted to show that the Shang kings were so evil that people should be thankful they were gone. It's possible that the accounts are basically true, but it's also possible that the writers either made up the negative stories, or at least exaggerated the worst parts.

In any case, because of evil rulers or for some other reason, it appeared that the Shangs' days were numbered. Out of nowhere, according to the *Bamboo Annals*, "A red bird perched on the Zhou altar of the soil." Red birds are rare, and to see one standing on a place holy to the rival Zhou state would be a cause of worry for the Shang. Were the heavens trying to tell them something?

66 Sima Qian, "Basic Annals," *Record of the Historian,* about 100 BCE

66 Sima Qian, "Basic Annals," *Record of the Historian,* about 100 BCE

ANIMAL YEARS

The Shang divided each day into 12 blocks of 2 hours each. Weeks were ten days long. Years went in cycles of 12. Instead of having a number, each year was associated with an animal. The Shang believed that people resembled the animal linked with the year in which they were born. For instance, dragons are the luckiest; tigers are powerful, strong-willed, and outspoken; and snakes are wise but don't talk much.

Horse	1990, 2002	Rat	1996, 2008
Goat	1991, 2003	Cow	1997, 2009
Monkey	1992, 2004	Tiger	1998, 2010
Chicken	1993, 2005	Rabbit	1999, 2011
Pig	1994, 2006	Dragon	2000, 2012
Dog	1995, 2007	Snake	2001, 2013

To find a year not on this list, add or subtract multiples of 12 to the years listed here.

The Chinese used this calendar until 1911. Chinese people still use it to determine the date of the New Year and other important events. New Year's Day is always on a new moon, but its exact date on the Western calendar varies from late January to early March.

Is the tiger devouring this man or protecting him? Is the man a human or a demon? Or is this a single creature, part human and part tiger? This bronze vessel from the Shang dynasty probably held some type of religious significance, but scholars disagree about its meaning.

ARCHAEOLOGIST AT WORK:
AN INTERVIEW WITH
ROBERT MUROWCHICK

Robert Murowchick is a research associate professor at Boston University's College of Arts and Sciences East Asian Archaeology Center. He has been part of an international archaeological team excavating in the North China Plain since 1991, when the Chinese government passed a law allowing foreign archaeologists to collaborate on digs in their country.

Where in China do you work?
A few hundred miles south of Beijing, in the far eastern part of Henan Province. This project was started by my teacher, K. C. Chang.

Do archaeologists from different countries work together there?
Yes, we have Chinese participants, and American participants, and Canadian participants—it's a lot of fun.

What's the North China Plain like?
It's flat. It's boring, physically. It's mostly wheat fields, some corn.

It's a fun project because it's mostly based on some ancient texts that talk about this capital city, Da Yi Shang, which literally means "Great City Shang."

That's pretty clear!
They didn't mess around with any romantic names for their cities! The texts talk about the importance of the city as the ritual center and the political center of the Shang state before it became the Shang dynasty, so this is a period that we call the predynastic Shang (about 1800–1700 BCE to 1500 BCE). After

the Shang dynasty becomes the real power in the area, it moves the capital city someplace else, but the ritual center supposedly stayed for many, many hundreds of years at Great City Shang. When the Zhou people overthrow the Shang dynasty, they burn the last capital city to the ground but they allow members of the Shang royal family to return to the site of Great City Shang to continue to make offerings to the Shang ancestors. This was real sacred space for some reason. And so, during the Western Zhou dynasty, according to the texts, the Shang leaders established a new city on the ruins of this old city, and this new city was called Song. And then the city Song was vastly expanded during the Eastern Zhou period and became quite a powerful city-state, and a new city was built on top of it in the Han dynasty, and then in later dynasties more cities were built on top of these other cities. For some reason they kept returning to this one spot and kept building on the ruins of these earlier cities.

Does that make it hard to excavate?
Well, this whole area is covered by these flood deposits from the river, so archaeology

is very difficult for any kind of project because of these very thick deposits from the Yellow River.

So why did you choose that particular area?
K. C. was so convinced that the early texts, which were written in the seventh or sixth century BCE, were accurate and precise in their descriptions that he really used the texts as a map.

In 1996 a team hit something really hard in the earth and as they dug through it, it turned out that this was the rammed-earth wall of one of these early cities. By the end of the next year we had this massive wall located on the map. It's something like nine times larger than the modern city that sits on it today.

We were very excited, but the local people knew all along that it was there. This was local history, and nobody doubted it.

The problem is that the earliest city that we're looking for, Great City Shang—we have no doubts that it's under there, but it's so deep, 35 feet below the surface, and the water table is only about 15 feet below the surface, so once you go deeper than the water table, the water runs into the hole and your walls collapse, and it's quite a dangerous situation.

So when you say you find a city what exactly do you find?
These aren't beautiful marble buildings. These are foundations of buildings and walls made of rammed earth. The city is surrounded by a massive rammed-earth wall that originally probably measured 40 feet thick by 40 feet high. Within that wall you would probably have streets and avenues, and there would be a governmental district, and residential districts, and workshops of various kinds. So it's not that different from cities of any ancient culture.

Have you found anything that changed how people thought about this time period?
Actually we have. Part of our team was excavating a late Neolithic (3000–2000 BCE) village site in the area, of a culture called the Longshan, and this village site actually provided some real surprises. One season the archaeologists were digging and they hit a cattle skull and as they excavated it, it turns out it was a sacrificial pit that contains nine intact cattle and one deer skull. This is the largest cattle sacrifice that's ever been found in Neolithic China.

And it's really neat to us because the Shang is the culture that follows this late Neolithic culture and the Shang made a lot of sacrifices of cattle to their ancestors. So here we have the late Neolithic people, just a few hundred years before the Shang, also putting great importance on this large-scale slaughter of cattle, so it gives us sort of a continuity through time. That was very unexpected.

So basically this project is going in two different directions. One is we're trying to find this predynastic period of Shang, but more broadly we're trying to get a sense of the cultures that precede it because this era is relatively little known archaeologically.

It ought to be a spectacular site, once we find it.

CHAPTER 6

❝ BOOK OF POETRY AND BOOK OF DOCUMENTS

"HEAVEN IS BRIGHTLY AWESOME"

THE WESTERN ZHOU ERA AND THE MANDATE OF HEAVEN

Few modern people can understand the shock that people must have felt when a new ruling family, the Zhou, overthrew the Shang dynasty. The Shang had ruled for centuries, so long that in the minds of the people they ruled, "king" equaled "Shang." The Shang kings were humanity's link to the gods, especially their royal ancestors. With someone else in power, people wondered, who would ask

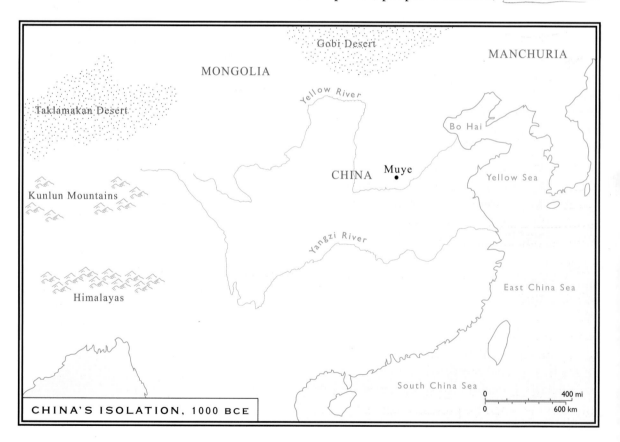

CHINA'S ISOLATION, 1000 BCE

the Shang ancestors for good weather for their crops? Who would find out the correct sacrifice? Some must have panicked, and many of them must have had a hard time understanding what it meant to have a new family in power.

And to make matters worse, many considered the new Zhou rulers to be foreigners. They were from the edge of the Shang world, and most of their new subjects thought of them as barbarians (the Shang viewed non-Chinese people as wild and uncivilized).

Exactly what was Chinese is hard to say. Mainly it meant people who had a similar language, which is the ancestor of the modern Chinese languages, and similar customs. People who considered themselves Chinese generally followed the same laws and spoke the same language when they went from one state to another. The boundaries between what was China and what was "other" kept shifting. Many states began as non-Chinese but later merged into Chinese culture.

The geography of China isolates the area and its inhabitants from its surroundings. The Himalayas to the west are steep and forbidding (the world's highest mountain, Mount Everest, is part of that chain). The plains of Mongolia and Manchuria to the north are still difficult to cross and were almost impassable until camels and horses were domesticated. The oceans on the east and part of the south were an even more difficult barrier for the early Chinese than the Great Wall of China was to become for invaders many centuries later. Only rarely did a very brave and very tough person from the outside manage to make it into China, and the few-and-far-between strangers were looked on with suspicion.

Exactly where the Zhou came from is unclear. Most scholars think that they originated in the high plains of central Shaanxi Province. But even though their home was far away, some members of the family managed to get involved with politics even before they took over ruling the country. One Zhou man, whose title, Wen, means "civilized," was even a high official in the Shang court. But Wen got himself into trouble when he protested against the last Shang king's evil deeds. He was thrown into jail for seven years. After

A DISCARDED BABY

The Zhou had their own theory about their origins. In the "Basic Annals" of the *Record of the Historian* of 100 BCE, Sima Qian recounts the story of a woman named Jiang Yuan who "went out into the wilderness and saw a giant footprint." She instantly became pregnant and realized that this was the mark of the great god Di.

When her baby was born, she thought he was unlucky and she "abandoned him on a narrow trail." But the livestock that passed by would not step on him. So she put him in a forest, but there were a lot of people there. She was worried that they might save him, so she abandoned him on the ice in a ditch, but there birds covered him with their wings.

Jiang Yuan thought he must be divine, so she gathered him up and raised him. Because she had at first wanted to discard him, she named him Qi, "Discarded." Qi is said to have founded the Ji clan that ruled the Zhou dynasty and also to have taught the Chinese how to grow crops.

Since the Western Zhou period, large Chinese houses and palaces have been made up of many rooms surrounding one or more courtyards. Families spent much of their time in the courtyards, where the sunlight made it possible for work to be done. The walls of the courtyard allowed women to work outside while still remaining beyond the gaze of non-relatives.

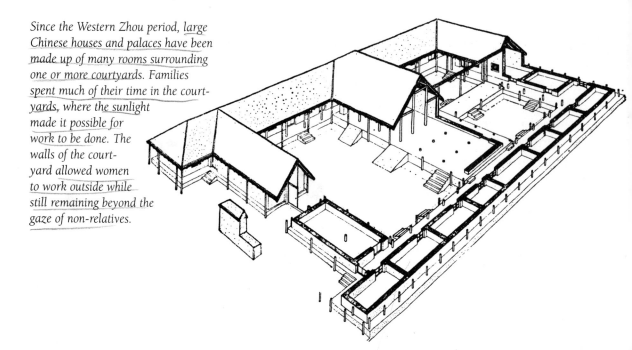

his release, Wen tried to convince other groups to join with him against the Shang, but he died before he could get anywhere.

Wen's son Wu was luckier. He gathered support from other people who wanted the Shang rule to end. He eventually led a large army (the *Record of the Historian* says that it was made up of 45,000 soldiers and 300 chariots) to victory over the Shang in the Battle of Muye, which took place 30 miles (50 kilometers) south of Anyang, in 1046 or 1045 BCE. The anonymous author of a poem in the seventh-century BCE *Book of Poetry* expressed the thrill that spectators must have felt in seeing the great victory:

[66] Anonymous, *Book of Poetry,* seventh century BCE

Vast was Shepherd's Field,
Our sandalwood chariots sparkled.
The team of four black-and-white horses so stately,
That is the general Shangfu.
He soars like an eagle
To aid that King Wu.
Launching an attack on the great Shang,
He encountered a clear bright morning.

When King Wu died two years later, his son Cheng was all set to inherit the throne. But there was a problem: One of Wu's brothers, the Duke of Zhou, argued that Cheng was too young, and said that he (the uncle) should rule for a few years. Some people objected, but the duke got his way. Modern historians aren't sure whether Cheng really was too young, or whether the duke was just trying to take over.

People later said that the Duke of Zhou had been a virtuous man. A story about the duke says that when his brother, King Wu, was still alive, the king became very ill. The duke was afraid that his brother would die and nobly offered his own life in his place, hoping that the forces in charge of life and death would make this switch. According to the anonymous *Book of Documents* compiled between about 1040 BCE and the seventh century BCE, when Cheng found out years later what his uncle had done, he said, "Heaven has stirred its awesome power to reveal the virtue of the Duke of Zhou."

Cheng did have some power, though, even while he was king only in name. He could wage war, for example. Once some of his uncles in the East rebelled against his rule, so he consulted the oracle bones to find out what the gods wanted. According to the reading of the bones, the gods wanted Cheng to start a war against those uncles. His counselors were nervous about attacking these powerful men, who had many supporters, and they advised him not to do it. But Cheng was convinced that the gods were on his side. "Heaven is brightly awesome," he said, according to the *Book of Documents*. "It helps our grand foundation." Cheng and his allies defeated the rebellious uncles, and after seven years, the uncle who had been ruling in Cheng's place finally turned over the throne to his nephew.

It looked as if **Heaven** really was on King Cheng's side. This was a perfect way to convince the people that the Zhou were legitimate rulers, and not barbarians from the west. If Heaven was with them, who would dare to be against them?

The concept of Heaven as a force that supported the king was new to China, but it was an idea that lasted a long time. The leaders saw this support as a mandate (a command

66 King Cheng, 11th-century BCE proclamation, in *Book of Documents*, 7th century BCE

66 King Cheng, 11th-century BCE proclamation, in *Book of Documents*, 7th century BCE

天

"tian" = heaven or sky; the dwelling-place of the gods; gods and ancestors who live in Heaven; or one high god

Because of King Wu's fame as founder of the great Zhou dynasty, artists were still making paintings of him more than 2,000 years after his reign. In this portrait he looks so imposing that even with his back turned toward the viewer, he still appears powerful.

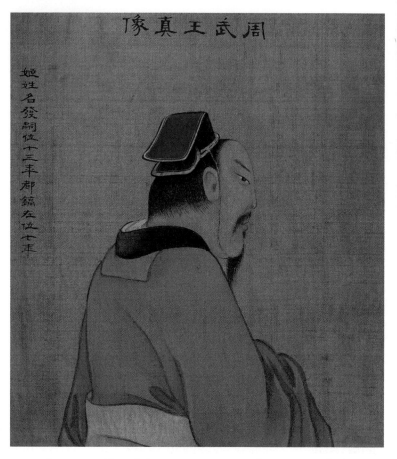

or order, usually giving someone authority to do something). Chinese rulers used the "Mandate of Heaven" for 30 centuries to justify their rule.

The Zhou said that the Shang had once had the Mandate, but that their bad behavior had caused them to lose it. King Cheng said in a proclamation,

King Cheng, 11th-century BCE proclamation, in *Book of Documents*, 7th century BCE

> The last ruler of the Shang was addicted to wine and believed he had the Mandate. He did not express concern for the people's troubles and he clung to old resentments and hatreds.... His heart was vicious and he did not fear death.... For this reason, Heaven sent destruction down on the Shang and did not aid them.

The notion of the Mandate of Heaven did more than convince people that the Zhou were justified in getting rid of the Shang. It changed Chinese religion, leading to a belief that the gods cared about what happened to ordinary people, since a ruler who treated his people badly might be seen as having lost the Mandate and would lose power. The belief also strengthened the king's position, since he was now considered the Son of Heaven, chosen not only to rule on earth but also to act as a go-between for Heaven and the people.

The Mandate also shaped the way Chinese people viewed leadership. Anyone who wanted to overthrow a ruler could claim that the leader had lost his Mandate and that it had passed to the person who wanted to take over. Belief in the Mandate made writers of history look for evidence that the last king in any dynasty was an evil person, and that the first king of the next dynasty was a virtuous leader whose success was proof that the Mandate had been transferred to him. Later historians called the pattern of a bad dynasty being replaced by a good one over and over again "the dynastic cycle."

For a long time it looked as though Heaven really was on the side of the Zhou. People became suspicious about their Mandate, however, when disasters started happening during the reign of King You. First there was a damaging earthquake. Then rivers dried up. Both the sun and the moon went into eclipse at different times. For people who had no idea what caused these natural occurrences, it looked as if the gods were saying that the whole universe—including the king's right to rule—was out of kilter.

It seemed that the Zhou were about to lose the Mandate of Heaven.

WATCH WHO YOU MESS WITH

King You's father, King Xuan, had some problems, too, including a run-in with an angry ghost. According to a ninth-century BCE text quoted in the fourth-century *Tales of the States,* the king had killed an innocent man named the Earl of Du. Three years later, the king went out hunting, but "at mid-day, the Earl of Du appeared on the left side of the road, wearing a red robe and cap, carrying a red bow and arrows. He shot the king in the heart, breaking his spine, and he died."

CHAPTER 7

WHO'S IN CHARGE?
THE RISE OF THE HEGEMONS

Wouldn't it be great to be a king during the Zhou dynasty? You would have a close relationship with both the gods and the spirits of your powerful dead ancestors. You would be the highest-ranking person in the entire land and nobody could tell you what to do. You would even have the stamp of approval from the gods—the Mandate of Heaven—that proved you were the rightful king. The perfect life, right?

Wrong. A king could lose the Mandate of Heaven, sometimes without warning. And although the king was on top of things, he had his lofty position only as long as he held the respect of the powerful military men who were right below him in the strict **hierarchy** that made up Zhou society. These lords supported the king with their soldiers and also gave him gifts—some symbolic of their allegiance,

A hierarchy is a system of ranking people or things.

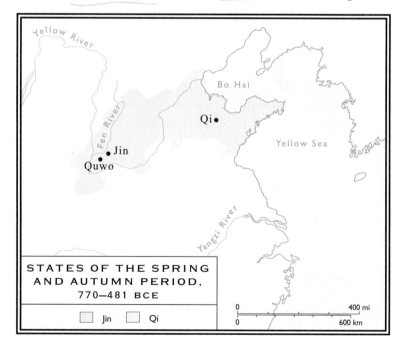

STATES OF THE SPRING
AND AUTUMN PERIOD,
770–481 BCE

Jin   Qi

0   400 mi
0   600 km

and some more practical. In exchange, the lords received the king's protection, both political and religious. But this relationship could crumble at any time, and then there would be trouble. Some of the lords had armies almost as large as the king's and they were accustomed to governing their own lands.

If a Zhou king was not a great leader and the lords lost respect for him, the king was in a shaky position. In the ninth century BCE, according to the *Record of the Historian*, a king named Li "acted cruelly and extravagantly. The people in the capital spoke of the king's faults." People probably spoke negatively of the king only in private, because in public, they were so terrified of him that they "dared not say a word, but only communicated by glances on the roads" for fear that one of his spies would catch them and they would be executed. This isn't the kind of behavior that would make the gods want to extend their Mandate for much longer.

So the kings' hold on power during the Eastern Zhou period (770–221 BCE) was not very firm. True, they belonged to the once-powerful Zhou dynasty, but unlike their ancestors, they weren't strong military leaders. Other states around the Zhou territory were quick to notice this lack of direction from the top, and the Zhou's subjects began to worry about invasion.

The situation became even more serious under the rule of King You. You (his name fit his personality—it means "in the dark") married a woman named Bao Si, the daughter of a nearby ruler. According to the *Record of the Historian*, "King You loved and doted on Bao Si." He pushed aside his first wife, the daughter of yet another ruler, and replaced her with the new one, declaring that the new wife's son would be his heir. Both of these acts were serious insults to his first wife and her family.

People knew that King You's actions would cause trouble. One of the king's officials said gloomily, "The calamity has taken form. There is nothing we can do about it." A rumor went around that Bao Si was not human at all, but was born from dragon spit.

Sima Qian, "Basic Annals," *Record of the Historian*, about 100 BCE

SPRING AND AUTUMN

During the Eastern Zhou period (770–221 BCE), the leaders of the Zhou dynasty ruled from a capital to the east of its original home. The first part of the era (770–481 BCE) is called the "Spring and Autumn" period, from the title of a history written during this period. The anonymous author of this history recorded important events by the seasons in which they occurred.

Sima Qian, "Basic Annals," *Record of the Historian*, about 100 BCE

The way the king behaved didn't improve matters. Once, someone thought that an enemy was attacking the capital. Sentinels lit signal lights to tell the lords to rush to defend the king—but there was no attack. These men looked foolish, galloping up with their armies, only to find there was nobody to fight. Bao Si was basically a sour-natured person, but at this sight, she burst out laughing. The king was so delighted to hear her rare laugh that he ordered the signal lights to be lit over and over, just to hear it again. The lords eventually stopped paying attention to the lights, and when they were lit in 771 BCE, everybody ignored them. But this time the attack was real, and King You was killed by invaders led by his first wife's father.

The capital was destroyed and some thought the dynasty would end. Instead, King You became the last king of the Western Zhou. The nobles helped his son, King Ping, establish a new capital in Luoyang, in the east, and he became the first king of the Eastern Zhou.

Over the next several decades, groups of people attacked states that had been loyal to the Zhou, and another royal family in the south was starting to act as if it wanted to take

similar to the boy who cried wolf [handwritten margin note]

DYNASTIES OF ANCIENT CHINA

1046–221 BCE
Zhou Dynasty

1046–777 BCE
Western Zhou

770–221 BCE
Eastern Zhou

770–481 BCE
Spring & Autumn Period

480–222 BCE
Warring States Period

221–206 BCE
Qin Dynasty

206 BCE–220 CE
Han Dynasty

over. Someone needed to step in and pull the different states together. The lords looked to Duke Huan of Qi. Qi was an ancient and wealthy land with a strong army. Part of its region is mountainous, and part is on the eastern coast, at the edge of the Chinese world.

On the other side of Qi's borders lived non-Chinese people whom the Qi considered barbarians. Dukes who owed allegiance to the Zhou kings ruled this territory. When a disagreement arose over who should take over after a duke died in 686 BCE, a talented official named Guan Zhong supported Jiu, the late duke's oldest brother, against a younger brother, Huan.

Taking sides like this was risky. If the person you supported won, everything was fine. But if he lost, he was usually killed and his supporters were supposed to commit suicide. Jiu lost, and he was executed by Huan's order. Everyone expected Guan Zhong to do the honorable thing and join his lord in death. But Guan shocked everyone when instead he turned himself in as a prisoner to Huan.

At first, Huan was furious at the man who had supported Jiu, saying, according to the *The Tradition of Zuo*, written in the late fourth century BCE, "Guan Zhong is my sworn

ONE IF BY LAND, TWO IF BY SEA

Since the Zhou states were constantly under the threat of attack, they set up an ingenious system of signal lights. They built towers close together so that sentinels in one tower could see the next. In case of attack, a watchman would light a flame. Guards in other towers would see the flame and light their own beacons, spreading the alarm.

  Anonymous, *The Tradition of Zuo*, about 300 BCE

Creating a set of bronze bells that played in tune required the skill of a group of highly trained craftspeople. The Marquis of Zeng, in whose tomb these bells were found, was one of a handful of people wealthy enough to afford a complete set.

enemy. I want him so that I can personally get my hands on him." And Huan had a personal reason for disliking this man: Guan had almost killed the duke in battle. The duke was saved only because Guan's arrow hit Huan's belt buckle. But one of Huan's ministers told the duke, "Guan Zhong is better at government than Gao Xi [Huan's former assistant]. You can use him as your minister." The duke changed his mind about revenge and took on Guan as his most important assistant.

Almost everyone was astonished. Guan had supported Duke Huan's enemy, so what made Huan think he could trust him? And at a time when men gained positions in the government through their noble birth, people were upset that Guan's only claim to his important job was that he was good at it.

Also, according to the codes of honor of the time, Guan had acted disgracefully by not committing suicide when the man he supported was killed. He defended himself by saying he had acted in his country's best interest. According to the third-century BCE book called *Master Guan,* Guan said, "It was because I wished to make the altars of Land and Grain [which stood for the state] secure that I did not die for Jiu."

Duke Huan made Guan Zhong his honorary uncle. That way it was all right for the duke to give his assistant houses, villages, and other gifts that technically he should have given only to members of the nobility.

The duke and his "uncle" ran Qi's government very efficiently. When fear of invasion made the states look for a military leader, they chose Huan. The person the lords chose to lead them during the crisis was called a "**hegemon**." Huan took the position of hegemon in 680 BCE and held it for almost 40 years, long after the original threat had passed. This was the first of five times that the lords appointed someone from their own ranks to take charge.

Some sources say that Duke Huan called the leaders of the allied states together nine times to settle disputes and to make alliances with each other, and to renew their vows of loyalty to the king. Each meeting was a combination of a religious rite and a political gathering and was run strictly, with a great deal of ritual and ceremony. After all of the

“ Anonymous, *The Tradition of Zuo,* about 300 BCE

“ Anonymous, *Master Guan,* written about 300 BCE but based on much older stories

霸

A hegemon is an overlord, or *ba* in Chinese.

leaders had agreed on what they were going to do, they ended with a solemn oath. Priests performed a sacrifice in a rectangular pit dug near the altar of the God of the Soil. The victim was usually an ox, although at least once, after Huan's rule had ended, a man was burned in the pit for arriving late at the meeting. They used the sacrificial victim's blood as ink to write their treaty, and then each of the leaders smeared the blood on his lips. This symbolized that their mouths had spoken truthfully.

Huan held his territory with a tight fist. He led the armies of his own state and those of his allies into battle. In fact, he was just like a king except that the Zhou king still had the religious powers that made him too important to ignore. All these duties made for a lot of work for one man. It was too much, in fact, and Duke Huan relied more and more on his right-hand man, Guan Zhong.

Later generations of Chinese had mixed opinions about Guan Zhong. Some criticized him for not killing himself when Prince Jiu died, for serving Duke Huan, who had ordered the death of his own brother, and for accepting what they considered inappropriate gifts from the duke. They also disapproved of his taking a high-ranking position in the government when he didn't belong to the social class that was supposed to fill that.

Others gave him credit for helping to keep Qi strong, and preventing people they despised as barbarians from taking over. The **philosopher** Confucius said in his *Analects* many years later: "Were it not for Guan Zhong, today we would be wearing our hair untied and would fasten our clothes on the left [like the barbarians]."

Even if some of them disapproved of Huan, many later Chinese writers admired this setup of a ruler assisted by an intelligent and hard-working assistant. But after the Spring and Autumn period, no one leader was strong enough to become a hegemon.

WHAT A BARBARIAN— HIS BUTTONS ARE ON THE WRONG SIDE!

Clothes and hairstyles help identify a person's culture and attitude. (This might have something to do with why parents sometimes object to the way their children dress and wear their hair.) A "civilized" ancient Chinese man had to wear his hair in a topknot and his clothes had to fasten on the right side, never the left.

A philosopher tries to understand the world and figure out what people should do to make society work smoothly. In China, a philosopher was someone with ideas about how individuals should act and how the ruler should govern his state.

❝ Confucius, *Analects,* fifth century BCE

CHAPTER 8

THE STORY OF SHENSHENG
SACRIFICE AND STATEHOOD

Adjusting to a stepparent can be difficult. Shensheng, the oldest son of Duke Xian of Jin, had more reason than most to be unhappy with his father's new wife.

Duke Xian ruled Jin, a state that owed allegiance to the Zhou rulers, from 676 to 651 BCE. The Zhou had founded this state, which was located between the Yellow River and the Fen River in what is now Shanxi Province. Jin was a barrier between the non-Chinese in its northern area and the Zhou capital due south, across the Yellow River. The people of Jin were a mix of groups, including the Rong, a tribe the Chinese considered barbarians.

Duke Xian had three sons, including Shensheng, when he went to war against the Rong. War was always dangerous, but it seemed as if even Heaven was against the duke in this one. His **diviner**, Su, had told Xian not to go, saying that the cracks on the oracle bones he used to tell the future looked ominous. Su said, according to the anonymous fourth-century BCE *Conversations of the States,*

> the crack...seems like a mouth holding a bone and the teeth...seem to be playing with the bone. They will gnash together, symbolizing alternating victory and defeat.... Moreover, I fear that if there are mouths [that say bad things about you], they will lead the people and the important families to transfer their allegiance from you.

Su's conclusion was, "You will win, but it will be unlucky." The duke went ahead with the war anyway. And at first it appeared that the diviner's gloomy reading of the cracks had been totally off base. Not only did Xian conquer his enemy, as expected, but he also brought home a new wife, a Rong princess who became known as Lady Li.

A diviner foretells the future, often by reading signs from nature or by interpreting the meaning of seemingly random events. Chinese diviners count sticks, toss coins, and use astrology and utterances from mediums to tell the future.

❝ Anonymous, *Conversations of the States,* fourth century BCE

The king's name is inscribed on this bronze cauldron. A descendant of the king's probably had the vessel made for use in sacrifices to his illustrious ancestor.

sacrificial vessel

At the feast celebrating his victory, Duke Xian told a servant to fill Su's cup with wine, but not to give him any of the meat from the animal that had been sacrificed to the gods as thanks for his success. According to the *Conversations of the States,* Xian denied Su the sacred food because his prophecy of bad luck had been false. "To defeat a state and obtain a wife," he said, "what could be luckier than this?"

Lady Li soon became the duke's favorite wife (men could have more than one wife, and rulers often had many), and they had a son. The idea that her child would never be duke because he had three older brothers bothered Li so much that she made up her mind to get rid of her stepsons. She started with Shensheng, saying things that cast doubts on his good character. Then she asked her husband to send the three brothers to rule far-off cities.

Anonymous, *Conversations of the States,* fourth century BCE

So now her three stepsons were out of the capital and some people were wondering whether the rumors she had spread about Shensheng were true. Then the duke put Shensheng in charge of an army that was invading another state. One of Duke Xian's knights was suspicious about this move. He thought it looked designed to harm Shensheng. If Shensheng was successful, he said, people would be envious and resentful of him, and if he lost, everyone would blame him for the failure. The knight warned Shensheng that his father was putting him in a no-win situation.

But Shensheng was virtuous. A virtuous man always obeyed the orders of his father and his lord, who happened, in Shensheng's case, to be the same person. He was victorious in this battle and then in another one against a different group of "barbarians." The knight was right; despite (or because of) these victories, the evil gossip that people were spreading about Shensheng grew worse.

Since her attempts to get her stepson killed off weren't succeeding, Lady Li tried **reverse psychology** on her husband. She went to the duke in tears and told him that Shensheng was a wonderful man—kind yet powerful, forgiving, compassionate—everything a son and a ruler should be. Lady Li told the duke that she was sure that Shensheng was concerned that his father's love for Li was distracting him from ruling his country. She said that her stepson was so honorable that concern for the state would make him try to take over his father's throne. Lady Li told the duke to kill her to remove this threat. The duke refused (Lady Li must have been relieved) and said he would take care of his son's ambition to rule. But Li's "noble" offer of self-sacrifice to save her husband's position must have made him suspicious of his oldest son, and even more confident of his wife.

Now that the duke's mind-set toward his son was mistrustful, it was time for Lady Li's final step. She told Shensheng, "Last night the ruler dreamt of Lady Jiang of Qi [Shensheng's mother]." In Chinese belief, a dead person would appear in a dream only when he or she was unhappy about something. Li told Shensheng that his mother's

Reverse psychology is convincing someone to do something by pretending you want them to do the opposite.

spirit must be restless, and that for her to rest in peace, he, the oldest son, "must quickly offer a sacrifice to her."

Sacrifice was an important way to coax the spirits of the dead to be favorable to the person performing the procedure. The ritual had two parts. First, food was prepared with a great deal of religious ceremony. A poem in the *Book of Poetry,* written in the seventh century BCE, shows how every step of the ritual was holy:

> In due order, treading carefully,
> We purify the oxen and sheep.
> We carry out the rice-offering, the harvest offering,
> Now baking, now boiling,
> Now setting out and arranging,
> Praying and sacrificing at the gate.

The food was then offered to the ancestral spirits.

66 Anonymous, *Conversations of the States,* fourth century BCE

66 Anonymous, *Book of Poetry,* seventh century BCE

Sacrifices to ancestors were solemn occasions. The participants followed precise guidelines about each detail of the ritual—the procedure, dress, and language—to ensure the success of the ceremony. Here, relatives offer food and drink to seven generations of ancestors.

THE AUGUST PERSONATOR

How do you sacrifice to someone who isn't there? One of the dead ancestor's grandsons (if the ancestor was a man) or grand-daughters-in-law (if the ancestor was a woman) would be chosen to act as his or her "personator," or stand-in. The personator was treated as the ghost of the dead person and would eat and drink the sacrificial offerings. The personator would then give blessings to the other participants in the ritual.

[66] Anonymous, *Conversations of the States,* fourth century BCE

The second part of the ritual was a feast where the descendants of the spirits shared the now-holy food among themselves and with their guests. It was a very special occasion, not only because it involved honoring one's ancestors, but also because people had a good meal, which was a luxury. Meat was expensive, and the only time that people were supposed to eat it was as part of a sacrifice.

A good son would not hesitate to perform the elaborate and costly sacrificial ritual. Despite his stepmother's rumors, Shensheng had always acted like a good son and a loyal subject. After all, he had risked his life and his reputation rather than disobey his father and his lord, even when a trusted official warned him against that action. He had gone off to rule Quwo, a faraway city, when his father ordered him there. So now that his dead mother appeared to be unhappy, he would do what a good son should do, and perform a sacrifice.

Lady Li had been very clever. She planned everything so that the duke would be away hunting when Shensheng arrived from Quwo with the blessed foods. She took advantage of her husband's absence, according to the *Conversations of the States,* to poison the wine and the meat. Then Duke Xian came home, and began the ritual by pouring wine on the earth:

> When the duke sacrificed some [wine] to the earth, the ground swelled up. Shensheng was frightened and left. Lady Li gave some of the meat to a dog and the dog died. She had a minor official drink some of the wine and he also died.

The Chinese of the Eastern Zhou period prized jewelry not only for its beauty, but also for its symbolic value. A ruler would wear a precious necklace during rituals to show off his wealth and power.

Shensheng knew that he was innocent of trying to poison his father, but he also knew that he would be blamed. If he maintained his innocence and people believed him, they would be angry with his father—something unthinkable for this dutiful son and subject. They might even think that his father, their leader, was the one who had poisoned the meat. His advisers urged him to flee out of the duke's reach. Shensheng refused, saying, "To abandon your lord to escape a criminal charge is to flee from death. . . . If the charges are proved, then leaving will make the crime worse. . . . Death cannot be avoided. I will await my fate."

So what could Shensheng do? Once again, he found himself in a no-win situation. If he ran away, he would shame his father, which a good son should never do, and betray his lord, which a good subject should never do. If he stayed, he would most likely be killed. To make matters worse, his stepmother

> came to see him and said, weeping, "If you can stand to do this to your father, what about the people of the state? . . . If you kill your father [by causing the people to lose confidence in him] . . . who will consider this a benefit? These actions are all despised by the citizens. It will be difficult for you to live long."

For a person of Shensheng's culture in such a situation, there was only one solution: suicide. He hanged himself in the temple. That way, he shamed no one and did not harm his father's reputation. Just before he took his life, he said, "I do not dare to regret my death."

An added benefit was that he could look forward to becoming a ghost and haunting his stepmother.

Shensheng's two other brothers evidently didn't suffer from as strong a conscience as he did. They both fled, and later wound up ruling the state of Jin. After Duke Xian died, supporters of the original three brothers killed Lady Li and her children, and the oldest surviving brother took the throne.

Historians are not sure how much of this story is true. While the major people involved certainly existed, parts of the story sound like a fairy tale: the three brothers, the vir-

Anonymous, Conversations of the States, fourth century BCE

Anonymous, Conversations of the States, fourth century BCE

A CHINESE CINDERELLA

A very old Chinese story is similar to the tale known in English as "Cinderella." After her father dies, a virtuous girl named Yexian is abused by her stepmother, who makes her do difficult and dangerous work. Yexian is saved by the bones of a magical fish to which she had been kind when it was alive. She prays to the bones for elegant clothes to attend a festival. When the stepsisters spot her at the festival, she hurries away, losing her golden slipper. The king is curious as to who could be the owner of such a beautiful shoe, and he has all the women in the kingdom try it on. When it fits Yexian, the king marries her.

tuous son, the wicked stepmother. It's possible that fact and fiction are intertwined in this tale, but unless an archaeologist stumbles upon documents that either support or dispute the facts, we will never know for sure.

Whether or not the details of the story of Shensheng are factually accurate, the way it praises virtues such as obedience and loyalty to one's father shows how important these values were in Chinese society at that time. Even though Shensheng knew he was being used by his evil stepmother and might end up dead because of it, he always obeyed his father without question and put his father's reputation above his own.

Being forced into suicide might not seem like much of a reward for good behavior, but in the Chinese belief system it was possible for Shensheng to get revenge later. While he was alive Shensheng did everything that a good and noble son should do, but once he became a spirit, he was no longer bound by earthly expectations. He was free to haunt and even harm those who had done him wrong. Many people must have thought that Shensheng's ghost was somehow involved in the death of the woman who had brought about his downfall and the children for whose sake she had behaved so treacherously.

The charcoal pieces in this portable cooking pot, found in the tomb of Marquis Yi of Zeng, were ready to be lit whenever the dead man became hungry.

CHAPTER 9

FROM BRONZE TO PLASTIC

CRAFTS IN EVERYDAY LIFE

What would you do with an empty box? If it's just something your shoes came in, you'd probably toss it in the recycling bin. But if it's a beautiful wooden box that your grandmother gave you for storing your treasures, you'd probably put it away someplace safe. If you forgot the box, it might stay hidden for a long time until somebody found it. If it was well made, it would survive the long years in your attic.

That's the situation with artifacts from ancient China. Because most of the artifacts that archaeologists have found are beautiful and well constructed, it would be easy for modern people admiring the ancient Chinese crafts in a museum to think that everything the ancient Chinese made and used was pretty to look at and well made. But the fact is that most of the more ordinary objects fell apart centuries ago. Common, everyday possessions of little value were often made of materials such as wood or animal hides, which wore out quickly and then disintegrated once people stopped taking care of them. This is why we see so few wooden spoons, work clothes, roughly made dishes, and similar objects from ancient China. People were more careful with their expensive possessions, which were also usually made of more durable materials.

Scholars know as little about the lives of ordinary people as they do about ordinary objects. Few details remain about the daily activities of the skilled artisans who produced the crafts that people relied on. But by looking at the items that remain and by reading the documents that have been discovered, historians can guess how someone who handled these crafts would have spent her day.

Imagine, for example, a maidservant in the house of the family of the Marquis Yi of Zeng (a marquis is a low-level

" Coffin of the Marquis of Zeng, Hubei Province, 433 BCE

The body of a powerful man such as Marquis Yi of Zeng would rest in several coffins, one inside the other. This inner coffin is made of lacquer and decorated with horned bird-men and fierce guards carrying weapons, who were intended to protect the body from evil spirits.

WIVES AND CONCUBINES

Powerful men in traditional China often had more than one wife, partly to show off that they were wealthy enough to support a large family, and partly to ensure that they would have a son to inherit their title and property. Unofficial wives were called concubines, and their sons could not inherit their father's title.

noble). In Hubei Province in 1977, archaeologists found his tomb, containing more than 10,000 treasures that dated from around 433 BCE. The state of Zeng is mysterious—it isn't mentioned in any historical sources.

Our maidservant, whom we can call Shuwan, might have been very young, perhaps as young as 13. She woke early so that she could have everything ready for when her mistress rose for the day. Her mistress was one of the wives or concubines of the marquis. The bodies of eight young women ages 13 to 24 were found in his tomb, so it appears that he had many female companions. Nothing more is known about them, not even their names.

On a cold morning, Shuwan would light a fire in a small portable stove. Perhaps she would prepare breakfast on it as well. The stove found in the marquis's tomb is made of bronze. The Chinese developed several methods for making complex and detailed pieces of this metal. The earliest examples in China of bronze made with a technique called the "lost-wax method" come from the marquis's tomb. Using this technique, a worker formed a model of the finished piece, but he made it of wax, not clay, as in the earlier "piece-mold" process. He shaped the wax around a core of some material that didn't melt. The artisan pressed clay onto the outside of the wax model and left it there to dry. Once the clay was hard, a workman poured hot bronze between the clay outer mold and the inner core, melting the wax (this is where the wax was "lost") and replacing it with the bronze, which hardened as it cooled. The metal took on the shape formed by the clay mold, which in turn reproduced the shape of the now lost wax model.

A worker then shattered the outer clay mold and removed the bronze object. This technique ensured that no two pieces produced by the lost-wax process could ever be identical. Some of the more complicated pieces in the tomb of the marquis were made from different pieces produced by the lost-wax process and joined together.

Bronze was valuable, and the workmanship that went into an intricate object was also costly. Each pot would have been worth a small fortune, and in the tomb of the Marquis of Zeng, archaeologists have found bronze objects weighing a total of over 22,000 pounds (10 metric tons)!

A maidservant would certainly have handled some of these fine objects in the course of her chores. Once her mistress was warmed and fed, Shuwan would help her to put on one of her fine silk gowns. Nobody knows exactly when silk was first produced in China, but by 1000 BCE the Chinese were already producing enough that they were trading it with other countries for their products.

Silk is made from the cocoons of silkworms (actually the larvae of a moth). Today most silk production is automated, but in the fifth century BCE, making a silk garment took the combined work of many people with different skills and training. The silkworms were carefully raised until they spun their cocoons. Each tiny cocoon, when unwound, could produce about a half-mile of silk thread. Different craftspeople then spun, dyed, and wove the thin fibers into cloth or used them to embroider beautiful designs on clothing or decorative hangings.

The marquis's wife no doubt wore fine jewelry as well. The Chinese prized jade, a semiprecious stone, for its beauty and for the way its fine grain could be carved into highly detailed forms. Chinese artists of the Neolithic Period (5000 to 2000 BCE) were already carving jade. The wife of the marquis, 3,000 years later, might have worn a pendant showing a complicated scene of two mythological animals twining around each other. A jade dagger found in the marquis's tomb was probably an ornament too, and not a real weapon, since the stone wouldn't

THE LOST LOST-WAX METHOD

For some reason, after a short time the Chinese forgot how to use the lost-wax method to create bronze objects and they didn't rediscover it for centuries.

The decorations on this wine server are the earliest known examples of the lost-wax method of bronze casting in China. This method allows craftspeople to make intricate details that would have been impossible with other techniques.

It's hard to imagine that a squirming mass of silkworms would produce delicate and lustrous silk. Silk made comfortable and beautiful garments and was so precious that it was used as money.

This brilliantly painted suitcase was as much proof of the owner's wealth as the clothes stored inside. Four men were needed to carry it, proving the suitcase's owner could afford servants just to carry his or his wife's belongings.

hold a sharp edge the way bronze or other metals could.

After her mistress was ready to start her day, Shuwan would have many duties to perform. Sometimes she would accompany her mistress on a journey. Perhaps the wife of the marquis was returning to her hometown to visit her parents. Maybe she was accompanying her husband on a diplomatic trip, or taking a trip to a sacred mountain to perform a sacrifice. In any case, the lady would have traveled with servants. They would take care of her and her possessions, and also show her hosts that her husband was wealthy enough to afford many people to work for his family.

Shuwan would pack everything her mistress needed for the trip. No ordinary box would do to hold the precious garments and jewelry of a fine lady. These suitcases may not look similar to what people travel with today, but their shape was practical at a time when you couldn't just open the trunk of a car and toss in your luggage. Travel was difficult, and servants would make the journey on foot. The handles would rest on the shoulders of the two men assigned to carry the case along the road, up mountains, and across rivers to its destination.

The suitcase looks like painted wood, but in fact, it's made of lacquer—an early form of plastic. Most people think of plastic as a modern invention, but by definition, any material that can be molded into a shape that it keeps once dry is a plastic. Lacquer starts off as a milky resin that comes from the lac tree, which is native to China and related to poison ivy. As the liquid dries, it turns sticky. A craftsman then spreads the liquid into a thin layer that hardens in about a day. As many as 1,000 layers are built up to form a hard, solid object that can then be turned into a work of art, a piece of furniture, a musical instrument, armor, or a suitcase. Lacquer is lightweight, hard, and water-resistant.

The marquis's double coffin is made of lacquer, as is the coffin of a dog found in his tomb. (Nobody knows why the dog is there.) Lacquer could also be turned into a hard, long-lasting paint. The lacquer paint on this suitcase is still bright and colorful after almost 2,500 years.

Before the lady departed, she might attend a banquet. Shuwan may have had time to grab a hasty bite as other servants prepared food and served it to the marquis's family and guests, perhaps using gold utensils. Gold isn't as practical as bronze—it's soft, for one thing—but it is even more expensive. A visitor seeing a humble object such as a soup bowl made of gold would be impressed by the marquis's incredible wealth.

After the meal ended, the marquis's wife and Shuwan would have departed on their journey, along with other servants and family members. No doubt they traveled with armed guards, as the contents of their boxes—and even the boxes themselves—represented more wealth than most people would expect to see in a lifetime of hard work.

We may never know how the people who worked for these wealthy lords and ladies, and the talented and highly trained craftspeople who created the beautiful objects that the wealthy used, felt about the differences in their lives. The proper relations between people of different status was just one of the questions that the great thinkers of Ancient China discussed. In the sixth century BCE a great man was born in China whose ideas about human nature and what makes a person good or bad still influence the thinking of people in China and many in the rest of world. His name was Confucius.

ETERNAL ROCK

Jade is so durable that for the ancient Chinese it seemed eternal and stood for immortality. Sometimes a person—a very wealthy person—was buried in a jade suit. More commonly, a small piece of jade would be put in a dead person's mouth.

CHAPTER 10

A WISE MAN AND HIS FOLLOWERS

CONFUCIUS AND CONFUCIANISM

❝ Confucius, *Analects*, fifth century BCE

"Is it not a joy to learn something, and then to use the knowledge from time to time?" "Don't worry about others not knowing about you; worry about you not knowing about others."

These are two statements made by the Chinese philosopher Confucius. Many people around the world have heard of Confucius and know that he was an ancient Chinese man who made wise statements about human beings. These people are partly right—but not completely.

First, people are only partly right about his name. It was not really Confucius, but Kong Qiu. His followers sometimes called him **Kongfuzi**, or "Great Master Kong." Catholic missionaries who went to China much later and admired his ideas referred to him by the Latin-sounding "Confucius."

It's also true that he said wise things. But Confucius did more

孔夫子

Kong + fu + zi = family name + title of respect + "master"

"The First Teacher, Confucius, spreading his teachings" is how the philosopher Confucius is identified in this illustration. "At home, be reverent; at work, be respectful; with friends, be loyal" is one of his sayings.

than write the proverbs that many people associate with him. He was a great thinker who was interested in how people ought to live, how society is structured, and how righteousness and justice can be achieved on earth. He influenced Chinese thought so deeply that his ideas and beliefs are still part of Chinese thinking today.

Confucius was born about 551 BCE into a China that was changing. In earlier times, the work that people did and the lives that they led were pretty much determined as soon as they were born. If your father worked for the king, you almost certainly would work for the next king when you grew up. If your parents were farmers, you would be a farmer someday. If you were the daughter of a silk weaver, one day you would learn how to weave silk.

But that rigid system was being challenged in the mid-sixth century BCE, even for the highest job in the land: ruler. Men who were not direct descendants of the oldest son of the last king made attempts to take over the throne. Also, the states were getting so large, and governing them was getting so complicated, that some rulers were taking the unusual step of relying on advice from men who were best able to help them govern, not necessarily the sons of earlier advisers. These new officials might come from families of soldiers, merchants, even farmers. All that mattered now was that they be talented and wealthy enough to afford the necessary education, and that they come to the attention of someone in power.

Along with these political and social changes came changes in religious customs. Ever since the long-ago days of the Shang dynasty, only the members of the royal family performed certain religious rituals. But now some other, non-royal men were starting to perform them.

Confucius came from one of the rising classes. His father was a knight of the state of Lu. Historians do not know who his mother was, and some think he was orphaned at an early age. You might expect that Confucius would be in favor of the new way of doing things, since it gave an advantage to men like him. Instead, he was horrified. He thought that the changes were dangerous for society, that they ruined

IF YOUR NAME IS HOPE, ARE YOU AN OPTIMIST?

Mencius, an important follower of Confucius, had an intriguing idea. He said that if people behaved the way their social positions were defined, everything would be well. For example, if a king is defined as someone who governs well, then someone who rules badly isn't truly a king, even if he is the son of the previous ruler. For this reason, Mencius said, you could kill the man who sits on the throne if he is a poor leader without being guilty of killing a king.

He also asserted that people are basically good. Why are there bad people, then? Well, Mencius said, water flows downhill. You can force it to run uphill with an external force, but it will go downhill whenever the force is removed. Similarly, circumstances can force people to be bad, but that doesn't change the fact that they are fundamentally good.

people's characters, and that the only way to get things back on the right track was to return to the way people had behaved in earlier generations.

Confucius had started out his career in a traditional way. He was an official in the government, and it doesn't appear that he was very successful, since he is mentioned only once in passing in documents of his time. A later document, the *Tradition of Zuo*, records that he held the position of Minister of Bandits (something like a sheriff).

Confucius found his real calling when he became a teacher. He grew so well known and his statements were so admired that before the first century BCE, his followers collected much of what he said in a book called the *Analects*. He ran his school with a mixture of tradition and innovation. A major innovation was that he would accept any man as a student (women had very little opportunity for any sort of education), regardless of social class, and he didn't care much about payment. A small bundle of dried meat was enough of a fee.

On the other hand, many of his methods looked traditional. In fact, Confucius claimed in the *Analects* that he was "a transmitter [of the old ways], not a creator [of new ones]." What was most traditional in his school was the course of study. Confucius's students learned the "six arts": archery, charioteering, ritual, music, **calligraphy**, and mathematics. His pupils studied literature as well. They were supposed to be tough, like true knights, and should follow the example of their teacher, who said, "I can live with coarse rice to eat, water for drink and my arm as a pillow and still be happy."

For Confucius, education wasn't as important as being a good member of society and of your family. He said, "A young man should be a dutiful son at home and be respectful to elders outside his home. He should be serious and trustworthy, loving all, but drawing close to the humane. After doing this, if he has energy to spare, he can study the literary arts."

Confucius cared deeply about decent behavior between people. His saying, "what you do not want for yourself, do

66 Confucius, *Analects*, fifth century BCE

calligraphy = "beautiful writing"
Calligraphy was an art form and a means of communication.

66 Confucius, *Analects*, fifth century BCE

66 Confucius, *Analects*, fifth century BCE

not inflict on others" is similar to the "Golden Rule": "Do unto others as you would have them do unto you."

Confucius was very much concerned with the duty that children owe their parents. He said that a son should cause so little trouble that "his parents have to worry only about him getting sick," not about misbehavior or any other kind of problem. He said that for at least three years after a father dies, his sons should keep doing things the same way that their father had done. Only then can they start making changes. If a parent behaves illegally or immorally, the children should gently try to change that parent's ways, but if that doesn't work, they should still respect their elders and honor their decisions.

Above all, people should behave with *ren*, or humanity, toward one another. This principle was so important to Confucius that he said that people should die rather than treat others badly.

What makes someone *ren*? Being honest and genuine with others is crucial. Confucius said that only someone who is "forceful, resolute, simple and cautious of speech" is truly noble of spirit, whereas one with "honeyed words and pious gestures" is not. Confucius even claimed that someone who is not *ren* cannot perform the important religious rituals that bound the Chinese people together. These rituals included ceremonies celebrating the return of spring, the harvest, the new year, and other important dates, as well as sacrifices to a family's dead ancestors. Confucius asked scornfully, "A man without humanity, what does he have to do with the rites?" Knowing the rites was important for a ruler. He said, "If you guide the people with laws and control them with punishments, they will avoid committing crimes, but have no personal sense of shame. If you guide them by means of virtue and control them with the rites, they will have a sense of shame and correct themselves."

A man who lives honorably, knows how to perform the rites, and cultivates *ren*, is a **junzi**—a gentleman. A *junzi* doesn't care much about his salary or about what people say about him. He doesn't just say the right things, but acts according to what he says.

PARTS OF SPEECH

Many words in classical Chinese can be different parts of speech without changing their form. *Ren* means not only "humanity" or "humaneness," but "humane" and "humanely."

66 Confucius, *Analects*, fifth century BCE

君子

Junzi = "son of the lord" The word was originally used for young nobles, but by this time had come to mean just "gentleman."

Confucius, *Analects*, fifth century BCE

Although Confucius was probably a strict teacher, many people found him appealing and even lovable. He was able to poke fun at himself, and he told one of his students that when someone asked what Confucius was like, he should say, "He is someone who forgets to eat when he gets excited about something, who is so happy that he forgets his troubles, and who doesn't realize that old age is upon him." He thought that people needed to take some responsibility for their own education and once said, "If a student is not eager, I won't teach him; if he does not struggle with the truth, I won't reveal it to him. If I lift up one corner and he can't come back with the other three, I will not do it again." In other words, Confucius would offer his students help on part of a problem and expect them to figure out the rest on their own.

Later philosophers and historians respected Confucius. Some said that he was so wise that he should have been a king. But others who started out following his teachings with devotion later broke away from strict Confucian teaching.

One of those who departed from the wise man's teachings was Mozi, who lived about a century after Confucius, and was probably even lower-born. He may have come from a family of carpenters (he used carpentry terms in his writings) or may have been a convict-laborer ("Mo" means "tattooed," and tattoos were sometimes used to mark convicts). At first, Mozi was a follower of Confucian ideas, but later he disagreed with much of what the earlier philosopher had said. Mozi was impatient at the emphasis Confucians laid on rituals and elaborate funerals, which Mozi thought wasted money that should have been spent on the living. He sought practical solutions to political and social problems.

Pupils studying with Confucius might learn how to play a qin, or lute, a stringed instrument plucked with the fingers.

Some of Mozi's ideas differed greatly from those of other thinkers of his day. For instance, he said that Heaven is interested in all individuals, not just the ruler. Heaven also, according to Mozi, has a plan, called the Will of Heaven, for each individual. Another new idea was that Heaven loves all people equally, and so should we. In the Confucian ideal, it's natural to love members of one's family more than strangers and people from your own country more than foreigners. Mozi rejected this, saying that loving some people more than others led to behavior that was against the Will of Heaven, such as stealing, heavy taxation, and injustice of all kinds.

Most of what scholars know about this philosopher comes from a fifth-century BCE book, the *Mozi*. This book contains some of his sayings, recorded by his followers, and also discusses nonphilosophical topics such as military tactics. Mozi was against warfare because it destroyed property, killed people, and often didn't give the winners the benefits that they were expecting. Besides, because Heaven loved everyone equally, Heaven would certainly be against anyone who was aggressive toward someone else. People and states could defend themselves from attack, he said, but they couldn't attack someone else.

Mozi didn't just say lofty things and then sit back and let other people put them into practice. Instead, he and his followers (called "Mohists") learned how to fight and offered their services to any small state that was being attacked by a larger one. Once, one of his followers was facing certain defeat in a battle. According to *Spring and Autumn Annals of Master Lü*, the philosopher said to the person who advised him to run away, "If I flee now, who will ever turn to the Mohists for help again?"

Mozi was only one of many philosophers whose ideas shaped the way Chinese people thought during the Warring States period (480–221 BCE) and in many cases, continue to think today. Among the most influential of these thinkers was the mysterious author of a book that still puzzles and inspires people all over the world today: the *Classic Text of the Way and Virtue*.

MORE OF CONFUCIUS'S SAYINGS

If someone is not humane, he cannot stand to dwell long in hardship or in good fortune.

If there is a knight/scholar who has his sights set on the right track but is ashamed of ugly clothes and poor food, he isn't worth talking to.

If I go walking with two others, there will certainly be one who can be my teacher. I select the good points of one and imitate them; I choose the bad points of the other and change them [in myself].

" *Spring and Autumn Annals of Master Lü*, about 240 BCE

CHAPTER 11

THE WAY
LAOZI

TIME TO MOVE ON

The *Record of the Historian*
tells us that Laozi
"observed the decline of
the Zhou and left." At that
time, large states were
attacking and sometimes
destroying smaller ones,
and no one paid much
attention to the Zhou king.

Imagine if a reporter wrote down a soccer coach's
pregame pep talk without mentioning that this was
advice given at a particular game. Someone reading the
coach's speech centuries later might think that the coach
was just talking in general, giving advice to people in any
situation of life. Parts of the pep talk would actually make
sense that way. "Work together as a team," "Plan ahead,"
and "Keep your eye on the goal" are good pieces of advice
in many areas of life, not just in soccer. But the future reader
might be confused by statements like "Keep fighting until
the whistle blows." Is this speech written for warriors about
to fight? the reader might wonder. If so, what does a whistle
have to do with it? And "This is our last chance against the
Tornadoes this season"—does that mean that everybody
gets a limited number of chances against violent storms
every season?

It's possible that something similar is going on with the
sayings in the book called the *Classic Text of the Way and
Virtue* (also sometimes called the *Laozi*, after its supposed
author). The statements in this text may be intended to
apply not to life in general, but to a specific situation.

Scholars have a lot of questions about the *Classic Text of
the Way and Virtue*. One central question is, who wrote it?
A legend says that an old man named Laozi was disgusted
with China and decided to leave. A border guard stopped
him and found out that the old man was a famous thinker
who wasn't planning to return from his journey. The guard
begged Laozi to leave behind his teachings for his country-
men. The old man complied, writing his ideas about *dao* or
tao (the Way) and *de* or *te* (virtue) in a book that became
known as the **Daodejing**, which can be translated as *Classic
Text of the Way and Virtue*. Then the old man left, and
"nobody knows what has become of him."

道德經

dao + de + jing = "the way" +
"virtue" + "scripture," "classic"

" Sima Qian, *Biography of
Laozi, Record of the Historian,*
about 100 BCE

People have wondered for a long time whether Laozi ever existed or if he was invented to provide the name of an author for the *Daodejing*. The *Record of the Historian*, a history book written in about 100 BCE, says that Laozi was an archivist (someone who took care of official records). The teacher Confucius went to Laozi to ask a question about rituals. Laozi dismissed the philosopher's concern with the rites and his interest in dead ancestors, saying, "Those of whom you speak have all already rotted away, both the men and their bones." Confucius, horrified at the man's lack of respect, reported to his friends, "Today I have seen Laozi; he is like a dragon!"

The author of that biography says that he tried to find out the true identity of Laozi. After getting three different responses, he gave up, saying he didn't know which to believe.

Modern scholars, like that ancient historian, also have questions about the author of this text. They agree that the Confucians made up the figure of Laozi in the Confucius story. Many historians think that in the original version, Confucius consulted the archivist, who should have known

This border guard is asking Laozi for a copy of his book. He kneels on a mat to show his respect for the great teacher and makes offerings to Laozi to thank him for the book.

❝ Sima Qian, "Biography of Laozi," *Record of the Historian*, about 100 BCE

better than anyone else how to perform rituals. In this way, the story makes Confucius look like a responsible person who took religion seriously. But as time went on, people who followed the teachings in the *Classic Text* gave a new twist to the story when they retold it. In the version in the *Record of the Historian,* the way the archivist scoffed at the rituals made the old traditions (and Confucius, who followed them) look silly.

Scholars also question whether the advice in the book was intended for life in general, or whether it was meant for a specific situation, like a coach's pep talk. So many of the statements in it look like criticisms of other philosophers of the time that some scholars think that at least some of it was written for a particular occasion or against a particular person.

Yet another mystery about the *Daodejing* is exactly when it was composed. Some of the confusion on this point was cleared up when Chinese archaeologists unearthed a tomb in south-central China in 1973. The archaeologists were able to date the tomb to no later than 168 BCE by looking at documents found in the tomb. These documents avoided using characters that are part of the emperor's name. The archaeologists were excited to find two silk scrolls on which the *Daodejing* was written. Until those scrolls were found, the earliest copy of this text known to modern scholars dated from about 500 CE. This one was far more ancient, which means that it might be closer to the original than the other versions known to scholars. Although the two parts of the book were reversed from the usual order (meaning that it should be called the *Dedaojing* instead of *Daodejing*), it agrees almost completely with the version that we have today.

In 1993 archaeologists found an even older copy, in a tomb from about 300 BCE. The text, written on three bundles of bamboo, is identical in many places with the commonly accepted version of the *Daodejing*. The portions of the book found on these bamboo slips may have been a kind of "greatest" hits of the *Daodejing*. with only highlights copied from the full text that is known today. But it could also be that this shorter work, which makes up about three-

GAIN A THRONE, LOSE A NAME

In China it was, and still is, disrespectful to call anyone by his or her name unless you are above that person in rank or age. You call your younger siblings by name, but your elders are "Older Sister" or "Older Brother."

Because no one was above the emperor, no one (except perhaps his mother) could call him by name. Once he came to the throne, nobody would use his name anymore. Instead, he would be referred to as "the current ruler" or "below the stairs"—his guards kept watch below the stairs, and everyone would pretend to communicate through them rather than directly with the emperor. If writings use the characters in an emperor's name, you know that they were written before he became emperor.

fifths of the standard text, was the complete original book, and that the rest was added later.

The text that scholars usually accept as the complete work today is divided into 81 chapters. Each has a few stanzas of lines that sometimes rhyme. Altogether, there are about 5,000 words in the entire book, which is a fairly short space into which the author packed a lot of wisdom—only about 20 typed pages, double-spaced, in English.

The *Daodejing* is made up mostly of short, catchy phrases that sound like proverbs. Several scholars have speculated that the book is based on popular sayings, and that some of

BEST-SELLER

Some people claim that the *Classic Text of the Way and Virtue* is the second-most commonly translated book in the world, after the Bible.

This rubbing from a Daoist sculpture shows the philosopher Laozi as a god. Rubbings are a way to see details that are hard to pick out on a worn, ancient stone. To make a rubbing, lay a piece of paper on top of a carving and rub a dark piece of charcoal or a crayon over the stone. The ancient Chinese used a soft bag dipped in ink.

MEANWHILE IN GREECE...

The philosopher Empedocles from the fifth century BCE said that combinations of four elements were the building blocks of everything on earth. Fire, in this system, was hot and dry, and was associated with males. Water was wet and cold, and associated with women. The other two elements were earth and air.

these sayings were common folk wisdom collected by whoever wrote the book. But the sayings strongly reflect the times, and they are negative about beliefs held by the Confucians (followers of the philosopher Confucius), Mohists (followers of the later philosopher Mozi), and Legalists (who believed in using harsh laws to control the people).

Of course, a book that exists just to put down its enemies will not last long once the enemies are no longer alive. The *Daodejing* contains more than that, and people continue to be inspired by such statements as:

- If you don't value rare goods, people won't become thieves.
- The world is a sacred vessel and cannot be controlled. If you try to control it, you will ruin it; if you try to seize it, you will lose it.
- Ruling a large state is like cooking a small fish [meaning you must do it carefully to avoid ruining it].
- I have three constant treasures which I embrace and treasure: The first is compassion, the second is frugality, the third is not putting myself ahead of the world.
- Sincere words are not beautiful and beautiful words are not sincere.

Many of the sayings have to do with the Dao—the Way. The author of the book admits that the Dao is impossible to define: "Those who know don't talk about it; those who talk don't know it." Even after centuries of discussion, there is little agreement on exactly what it means. It can be seen as a pattern or plan to the universe, or as a force midway between God and Nature. It is the mother of all things, and "the beginning of Heaven and Earth." The Way is even more important than the ruler, who comes fourth in a list: "The Way is great; Heaven is great; Earth is great; and the king is also great. In the country there are four greats, and the king occupies one place among them." The Way brings peace: "When the world has the Way, racehorses are retired to fertilize fields. When the world lacks the Way, war horses

Sayings in Daodejing

66 Anonymous, *Laozi*, third century BCE

are born in the suburbs." Even demons lose their ability to terrorize humanity: "If you rule the world through the Way, demons will have no magical power. It isn't really that they will have no magical power, but their magical power won't be able to harm people."

The reason the Way is so powerful, according to the *Daodejing,* is that it never acts for a purpose. It behaves so naturally that it is even called "nonaction." The great thing about nonaction is that you can "do nothing and yet everything will be done." Even a ruler should behave so that nobody feels his rule too heavily: "The subjects of the best kind of ruler only know there is such a person; those of the

The gods of Blessing, Success, and Long Life look at a painting of the Daoist symbol for Yin and Yang, the two opposite but complementary forces at work in the universe.

next best kind of ruler love and praise him; those of the next best fear him; and the subjects of the worst despise him." So the *second*-best kind of ruler is loved. The best is one that might as well not be there.

What kind of state would this ideal ruler govern? There would be no war, and each state would be self-sufficient. Some of the *Daodejing's* political thinking can be disturbing to modern people. In the state run by someone who rules with the Way, people are not supposed to think for themselves; instead, the king should "empty the minds and fill the bellies" of the people because "the reason why people are difficult to rule is because of their knowledge."

Another thought that may seem odd to modern and non-Chinese minds is the way the *Daodejing* praises weakness. According to this way of thinking, the weaker element (*yin*) is often preferable to the stronger (*yang*). This is especially strange because almost everybody in China at that time assumed that women were weaker than men outside the home (women were the bosses in the family). So by praising *yin*, some of the book's statements praise women— a highly unusual situation for the time. "The female [weaker side] constantly overcomes the male [stronger side] with tranquility." "When you know the male yet remember the female," runs the advice, "you'll be the ravine of the country." (A ravine is strong since it's a deep valley where rivers collect, making it more powerful than the imposing-looking mountain.) Everything is made up of two forces, the active, male *yang* and the passive, female *yin*. When one of them grows stronger, the other weakens, until they switch places.

The Dao is a way of peace, of finding balance, not only between *yin* and *yang*, but in all areas of life. But peace was a rare occurrence in ancient China. For most of its history, the land was at war, and much of China's wealth and energy was spent on keeping out invaders and defending the throne from would-be rulers.

Anonymous, *Laozi,* third century BCE

Anonymous, *Laozi,* third century BCE

CHAPTER 12

THE ART OF WAR

WARFARE IN ANCIENT CHINA

It would probably be good for humankind if more people could spend time like the Chinese philosophers, wondering about life and trying to figure out the best way to behave. Unfortunately, in ancient China as in most societies, conflicts often arose between people, and many times those conflicts were settled by war. The ancient Chinese states frequently fought against each other and against outsiders, so while some people were thinking about how to get along, many others were coming up with ways to conquer their neighbors.

War took a lot of resources. Men left their normal work to become soldiers, leading to labor shortages. The soldiers had to eat, but they weren't doing work that produced food. Soldiers needed weapons, and some of them also had to have armor and other expensive equipment. Wealthy fighters could buy these arms without too much financial strain, but it was a hardship for many families to lose their wage earner and then have to spend a lot equipping him for battle. So inventors and

Although a mere common soldier, this young man appears proud to be holding up the set of bells found in the tomb of Marquis Yi of Zeng.

A strategist is a person who plans how to carry out a military operation.

strategists had a real incentive to come up with better weapons and more efficient ways to fight.

One tool that gave early Chinese soldiers an edge over the competition was the chariot, which entered China sometime between 1600 and 1450 BCE, during the Shang dynasty. Each chariot could hold three men, and at first ten men went along on foot with each one. Chariots worked well on the flat North China Plain, but South China is covered with mountains, rivers, and lakes. So in those areas where driving a wheeled vehicle was difficult, another invention helped soldiers who were fighting at close range: the sword. Innovations in bronze working led to swords that could hold a sharp edge. These weapons were prized and many had beautiful decorations.

Rulers during the Western Zhou period (about 1045–771 BCE) had a lot to fight for. The first members of the dynasty had taken the throne from the Shang by force, and they knew that many people resented their rule and would have been happy to have someone else in power. The Zhou leaders also knew that there was a chance that the states around them might join together to fight against them as a unified force. So in order to protect themselves and to gain even more power by expanding their kingdom, they strengthened their armies.

The way wars were carried out started to change during the Spring and Autumn period (770–481 BCE). Before, warfare had followed a set of strictly defined rules. First, leaders of the opposing sides would issue challenges to each other until they agreed to fight. Drummers would beat out stirring rhythms to excite the soldiers, and then the armies would attack. Both sides followed certain rules of fair play, such as not attacking at night. Each army was supposed to have up to 1,000 chariots, for a total of more than 10,000 soldiers. Foot soldiers armed with spears and daggers accompanied the chariots.

As conflicts increased, the military became too large and too important to be run by people who just happened to have been born into families that traditionally supplied war leaders. Kings began choosing commanders based on their

This bronze flask was probably used to serve warm wine and could be hung from the chain attached to the handle. The bird on the stopper and carvings around the base are examples of the skill of the creator.

qualifications, not their birth. One of these strategists was Sun Wu, also known as Sunzi (Master Sun), who wrote *The Art of War* in the fifth century BCE. This book has long been a favorite of military leaders, including Mao Zedong, the leader of a revolution that toppled the Chinese government in the mid-20th century. He studied it to learn tactics of **guerrilla** warfare.

Sun Wu had many thoughts about how to be victorious in war. Some of them are:

- Warfare is the Way of Deception. If you are capable of accomplishing something, seem incapable; if you are close, seem distant; if you are distant, seem close.

- Know the enemy and know yourself, and you can fight a hundred battles with no danger of defeat.

- He will win who knows when to fight and when not to fight.

- Attack him where he is unprepared, appear where you are not expected.

- One cartload of the enemy's provisions is equivalent to twenty of one's own.

- To fight and conquer in all your battles is not supreme excellence; supreme excellence consists in breaking the enemy's resistance without fighting.

LEARNING FROM THE ANCIENTS

Since 2002 *The Art of War* has been translated into English at least five times. In 1999 an author named Gerald Michaelson examined how Sun Wu's advice could be applied to business. His book, *Sun Tzu: The Art of War for Managers*, was a best-seller.

guerrilla = "little war" in Spanish
An unofficial or semi-official war carried out by small, independent groups or a fighter in one of those wars.

Sun Wu, *The Art of War*, fifth century BCE

guerilla warfare

Sun Wu didn't just sit around thinking of things to say about war—he put his ideas into practice. The earliest surviving story about Sun Wu says that a king asked him if he could demonstrate his theories, even using women as soldiers (women were considered unfit to fight). Sun Wu responded by dividing the ladies of the court into two groups, each led by one of the king's favorite women. He then gave them orders, and when they burst out laughing, he had the two leaders beheaded. Not surprisingly, after that the surviving women did whatever he told them to do.

With men such as Sun Wu in charge of strategy and with advances in weaponry, war became more deadly. And as states grew more powerful and more wealthy, they had more money to spend on their armed forces, leading to large numbers of casualties. In a single battle in 341 BCE, the loser could expect 100,000 of his soldiers to be killed. This was already a huge loss, but by 295 BCE that number more than doubled to 240,000. In just one more generation—260 BCE—the number again rose dramatically, to 450,000. The winners also lost many soldiers, but nobody took an accurate count of them. The winners would cut off the left ear of each dead enemy, and then would count the ears to make the final tally.

Naturally, this slaughter alarmed everyone, not just soldiers and their military commanders. Leaders ordered large walls built across the countryside to slow down the advance of enemy troops, and existing walls around cities were strengthened and enlarged. A drawback to these walls was that while they kept attackers out, they also kept people in, so an army could surround a city and starve its inhabitants into submission.

Soldiers also worked hard at protecting themselves. Although the Chinese were experts at working bronze, the metal was too heavy and too expensive to be practical for a full set of armor. Most soldiers relied on thick pieces of leather stitched together. They needed good protection, because the weapons in use were very effective. Imagine a spear, with a straight blade sticking out the front, and then a second razor-sharp blade pointing straight out from the side,

ENOUGH IS ENOUGH

Sometimes combat was carried out for personal reasons. Men lived under a strict moral code that ordered them to seek vengeance for wrongs done to them or their families, and feuds might last for generations. The second-century BCE *Record of Rites* is clear about the need for revenge, saying: "Do not share the same sky with the mortal enemy of your father." When a king unjustly killed a man in the sixth century BCE, the murdered man's son was thirsty for vengeance. For this and other reasons, he waged war against the king. He won, but by then the king was already dead. This didn't stop his revenge, though—he ordered that the body be dug up and gave it 300 lashes with a whip.

and you'll be picturing the fierce dagger-lance. A soldier would swing it in a large arc to build up speed to strike his enemy. It's hard to believe that these garments offered much protection against such weapons. The application of a layer of lacquer would strengthen them further, but when the powerful crossbow was invented, these materials were not strong enough, and metal armor became a necessity.

Chinese horses were small and were mostly used for pulling chariots in teams. In the late fourth century BCE nomadic people from the north began making raids into China on horseback. The king who ruled the state closest to these tribes was impressed at how efficiently a cavalry (armed soldiers on horseback) could move, and he ordered mounted troops in his own army.

People were constantly coming up with ways to improve weaponry, tactics, and equipment. If these warring states somehow managed to come together as one country, and if these great minds would work on peace rather than on war, perhaps things would calm down.

Or would they?

King Gou Jian of Yue, who owned this sword, prized bronze weapons not only for their use-fulness but also for their beauty.

CHAPTER 13

CHINA GOES IMPERIAL
THE RISE OF THE UNIFIED STATE

It's sometimes dangerous to be too good at your job. An official named Shang Yang found this out when he was sentenced to a horrible death after trying to make laws more fair.

The state of Qin was in the northwest corner of what was then China, meaning the area where people spoke the Chinese language and observed Chinese customs. The borders of this China were constantly shifting, and in Shang Yang's time, Qin was just barely inside them. Qin was an area of high, dry, dusty plains, whose ruler relied on a prime minister to handle much of his administrative work. In the second half of the fourth century BCE, the Duke of Qin's right-hand man was his prime minister, Shang Yang. Shang Yang made many changes to improve the way Qin was run. One of the most important was a requirement that the law must apply to everybody, no matter how high the status of a lawbreaker.

The First Emperor of Qin was buried with a powerful army made of clay whose soldiers would defend him and his tomb after his death. The army included cavalry and horse-drawn carriages to drive off any ghostly invaders.

So when the duke's oldest son and heir committed a crime, Shang Yang had a problem. The law said that the young man should be punished, but another law said that "the heir could not be mutilated." Instead, Shang Yang ordered the young man's tutor to be punished severely. The duke's son was deeply offended at this insult to his tutor, and when he became duke he had his revenge: Shang Yang's limbs were tied to four chariots that then raced off in different directions, tearing him apart in front of a crowd in the marketplace.

But before he died, Shang Yang had made some important changes in how the state was run. He established rewards for reporting criminals, military promotion based on merit (not on birth or favoritism), and reforms in local government. He standardized weights and measurements, so that something weighing a *jin* in one part of Qin, for example, would weigh a *jin* in any other part of Qin. A new ruler, Ying Zheng, took over as king (the title had changed from "duke" to "king" in the fourth century) almost 100 years later. At that time, Qin was running more smoothly and more prosperously than most of its neighbors. This was thanks in great part to the efforts of a man who had been executed as a consequence of his own reforms.

By the time Ying Zheng was three years old, members of his family had taken over the last of the land that the formerly powerful Zhou clan had controlled. When he grew up, his appearance reflected his strong personality. According to an eyewitness description in the *Record of the Historian,* "The ruler of Qin has a big nose, long eyes, a powerful chest like that of a bird of prey, and the voice of a jackal. He rarely does anyone a favor and has the heart of a tiger or wolf."

Ying Zheng had to get to work right away, putting down a revolt when he took the throne at age thirteen. When he had taken care of that, he settled down to the business of war, conquering his neighboring states during the 220s BCE.

Understandably, the people in those other states weren't thrilled at being conquered. Prince Dan, who was next in line for the throne of the state of Yan, also had a personal reason for hating Ying Zheng. The two men had gotten to

<blockquote>Sima Qian, "Basic Annals," Record of the Historian, about 100 BCE</blockquote>

斤
A *jin* is about one pound, or half a kilogram.

HOW DO YOU SAY "CHINA"?

In modern Chinese, the land of China is called *zhongguo,* 中國 or Central Kingdom (as in "Center of the Earth"). The ancient Chinese people used the words *hua* 華 ("flowery") and *xia* 夏 (the name of the first dynasty) to refer to their land. Even today, the Chinese sometimes refer to themselves as *huaren* 華人 ("flowery people"). The name used in many other languages derives from Qin (秦) (also spelled Ch'in), since it was under the Qin rulers that China as we know it today was born.

know each other as boys when they were hostages in another state. You would think that this would lead to a lifelong friendship, but once Ying Zheng had become King of Qin, Prince Dan became his hostage. The prince wasn't happy with the way Ying Zheng treated him. He managed to flee home to Yan, where he plotted a way to get revenge and eliminate the threat to his country's independence. He came up with a plan: he sent an assassin named Jing Ke to kill Ying Zheng. Jing Ke "loved reading and swordplay," according to the *Record of the Historian*. Maybe his love of reading gave him the imagination necessary for the ingenious plot he hatched to get close to the king.

Jing Ke told a former Qin general, who now hated the king, that he had a plan to assassinate Ying Zheng. He needed an excuse to approach the throne, and his brilliant idea was to carry the general's head in a box to the king to prove that this enemy had been killed.

You might think that the general would prefer some other plan. But he was overjoyed at the thought that his death could help get rid of his hated enemy. According to the account, he said, "'Day and night I have gnashed my

Sima Qian, "Biography of Assassins," *Record of the Historian,* about 100 BCE

Sima Qian, "Biography of Assassins," *Record of the Historian,* about 100 BCE

The Qin government issued standard weights, such as this one made of bronze, which reassured people that trade was fair.

teeth and seared my heart for such a plan. At last I have been able to hear of it.' Then he slit his [own] throat."

Sure enough, Ying Zheng was so pleased at the sight of his enemy's head in a box that he allowed Jing Ke to approach him. But then "Jing Ke seized the king's sleeve with his left hand," says the *Record of the Historian*, "and with his right he picked up a dagger and stabbed at his chest. Before it reached his goal, the king...pulled himself to his feet, so that his sleeve tore away." Jing Ke chased the king around the throne room and threw his knife at him, but it struck a pillar. His attendants weren't allowed to carry weapons, so it took a while before they finally killed the would-be assassin, after which "the king sulked for some time."

Ying Zheng then brutally conquered Yan and much of the rest of China, making him the first Chinese emperor. He became known as Shi Huangdi, or "First Emperor."

After he had unified these different states into the Chinese Empire, Shi Huangdi continued the reforms that Shang Yang had begun a century earlier. Three of his more important accomplishments were the standardization of Chinese writing, so that people all over the empire could read what everybody else wrote, no matter what type of Chinese they spoke; direct rule from a central government, so that the laws were the same all over the empire; and the establishment of standard weights and measures and standard cart-widths (so that carts could all fit on the same roads).

Some of the First Emperor's actions might not look advanced to people today. For instance, some philosophical writings told the emperor how to behave, and Shi Huangdi thought this was improper. So he ordered the burning of all nontechnical books (he did keep a copy of each for the imperial library). When the book burning wasn't enough to keep the scholars quiet, he ordered 400 of them buried alive. After this most of the scholars stopped giving advice to the emperor and turned their thoughts to other matters.

Long before Shi Huangdi died in 209 BCE, he ordered the construction of his own **mausoleum**. An enormous labor force spent 40 years building the huge structure. The historian Sima Qian said in the "Basic Annals" that the First Emperor

“ Sima Qian, "Biography of Assassins," *Record of the Historian,* about 100 BCE

failedattempt

PLEASE OBEY THE TREATY, DAD!

States often exchanged hostages—frequently the sons of rulers or high officers—to make sure that their relationships stayed friendly. If a treaty or other agreement was broken, the hostage could be killed. Sometimes a defeated state would send hostages to the winner, probably to guarantee that they would follow the terms of their surrender.

Named for King Mausolus of Caria (now part of Turkey), whose wife had an elaborate tomb built for him, a mausoleum is a structure containing the bodies or coffins of one or more people.

“ Sima Qian, "Basic Annals,"
Record of the Historian, about
100 BCE

assembled more than 700,000 convict laborers from all over China. They dug through three springs, sealing them with molten bronze. They filled it [the mausoleum] with palaces, towers, and the hundred officials [perhaps statues of warriors] as well as marvelous devices and precious rarities. He ordered the craftsmen to make booby-trapped crossbows so that anyone who bored into [the mausoleum] would be shot.

The next emperor ordered the execution of Shi Huangdi's wives and concubines who had not had sons, and all the craftsmen and workers who had worked on the tomb were buried alive in it.

Skip ahead more than 2,000 years to the spring of 1974. Much of China was suffering from drought that year and people near the city of Xi'an in central China were digging a hole in hopes of finding an underground spring for a new well. Instead they came upon a terracotta (hard-baked pottery) head. Chinese archaeologists knew that Shi Huangdi had been buried nearby, so they hoped that they might find artifacts from his tomb. Perhaps this head belonged to the emperor's funeral goods, buried along with him to serve him in the next life. They began to excavate in earnest.

After years of digging, archaeologists unearthed more than 1,000 warrior statues, as well as statues of many horses and some chariots. The statues stand in the same formation that the members of a living army would take. The artists who crafted them took some effort to make them look like individuals, mixing and matching noses, eyes, facial hair, and other features. They stand in different poses: at attention, poised to attack, kneeling to draw a bow. Their clothing differs, often reflecting their rank or their position in the army, such as archery or infantry.

In 1995 archaeologists made a puzzling discovery: a fourth pit, carefully dug in a similar fashion to the three pits they had already excavated, was empty. Some scholars speculate that this pit was intended for the burial of living humans, not statues. Perhaps the emperor suddenly needed

IMPERIAL POWER

An emperor or empress rules an empire, a political unit made up of separate countries. Sometimes these countries may govern themselves, at least in part, but sometimes they become consolidated under one government. This was the case in China under the Qin. The title that Ying Zheng chose was brand new. He took *huang* (majesty) from the legendary Three Majesties (*sanhuang*) who ruled the world at the beginning of time, and *di,* meaning "god" from the ancient rulers called the Five Gods (*wudi*). His new word, which is translated into English as "emperor," means majestic god.

soldiers and decided that the men who had been destined to serve him in the afterlife might turn out to be more useful in the present world.

Modern people interested in these statues can see a replica in an unexpected place: the town of Katy, Texas, a suburb of Houston. Miniature reproductions of the terracotta statues stand in rows inside holes in the ground shaped like the First Emperor's burial pits. Even in miniature, the exhibit (which includes a copy of the emperor's palace complex) is the size of several football fields. The large numbers of tourists who visit this attraction show that this long-dead culture still fascinates many people.

The First Emperor had an entire army of terracotta soldiers buried near his tomb to protect it after his death. In earlier times, human beings (some of them while still alive), and not just statues, were buried with dead rulers.

CHAPTER 14

KINGS AND COMMONERS
LIU BANG AND THE FOUNDING OF THE HAN DYNASTY

If a woman dreams about a god and if her husband sees a dragon hovering over her body, you can bet that their son will be something special. If that boy later risks his own safety to kill a poisonous snake, there's no doubt left: this kid is marked for greatness.

That was the case with a man named Liu Bang. Liu needed all the supernatural help that he could get, because when he grew up he did something nobody had ever done before, something that horrified many people—although he was only a peasant, he became the emperor of China.

In 256 BCE, when Liu was born, the Chinese people were watching the Qin family become a powerful dynasty. The king of Qin conquered the other rulers in neighboring states and became Shi Huangdi, First Emperor. He left a note to be read after his death that said he wanted his son Fusu to be the next ruler. A courtier named Zhao Gao, however, preferred a weak ruler whom he could manipulate into doing what he wanted. He destroyed the late emperor's note and forged another one that ordered Fusu to commit suicide. Zhao Gao then said that Shi Huangdi actually had wanted Huhai, another of his sons, to be the next ruler. Huhai, who was in on the plot, stepped up to the throne.

The movie Farewell My Concubine *tells the story of modern actors portraying the story of the valiant general Xiang Yu (on the left) and his heroic death.*

Huhai wasn't too bright, and Zhao Gao wanted to show people that he could control the new emperor. He brought a deer to court and had everyone swear it was a horse. Huhai was bewildered. It just didn't look like a horse to him. But everyone else said that it was, so he figured he must have gone crazy and he agreed that it was a horse. This lack of self-confidence convinced Zhao Gao and the onlookers that Huhai was someone he could control easily.

Some people weren't happy with the Qin's firm grip on the country. They disliked the harsh laws, the high taxes, and the emperor's frequent demands that people leave their daily lives to build roads, walls, and palaces. Huhai's hold on the throne was starting to grow shaky, and if a few strong men came forward, he would have trouble holding on to it.

That's exactly what happened only a few years after Huhai became the second emperor. Several men plotted to get rid of him and his followers. Two of the most important rebels were Xiang Yu, the head of an old military family who led a group of dissatisfied aristocrats, and Chen She, a leader of peasants and workers.

Meanwhile, Liu Bang was living a comfortable and successful life in Pei, in eastern China. He had such a favorable appearance that a man who claimed to be able to read people's characters from their faces allowed him to marry his daughter, despite his wife's objections. Liu became a leader of a **ting**. Things were looking good for this peasant.

{ 停
A *ting* is a group of small villages.

Then disaster struck. One of Liu's jobs as *ting* leader was to escort groups of convicts to workplaces in need of labor. On the way to work at the site of the emperor's tomb, some of the convicts ran away. Now Liu was in big trouble. He knew that if he stopped to look for them, he would be beheaded for arriving late. On the other hand, if he appeared at the emperor's tomb site without all the workers, he would be executed for letting them escape.

Liu saw only one solution. He too ran away. He hid out in the bush and became a bandit, in charge of a group of men who did not support the emperor. Others joined him, attracted by his reputation as a kind and good leader. The first-century CE *History of the Han* says that Liu Bang "did not cultivate literary pursuits, but was by nature bright and understanding. He was adept at planning and could listen to others. From troops guarding the gates and garrison soldiers on up, he greeted them like old friends." A man like this was bound to have loyal followers.

Meanwhile, things were falling apart all over China. Chen She, the leader of the rebellious peasants, declared he was the King of Zhang-Chu. (Actually, there wasn't really any such state. Its territory was probably whatever land his army could occupy at any given time.) He looked like a real threat to the emperor until his charioteer killed him in 208 BCE.

People in Liu's home province of Pei rose up against the Qin rulers. They needed a leader. Who better than Liu Bang, whom everybody liked and who already had thousands of followers? They asked Liu to lead them, and he accepted. Xiang Yu, who led the disgruntled aristocrats, wasn't going to sit by and let these commoners take over the empire, so he decided to do it himself.

66 Ban Gu, *History of the Han,* first century CE

Wealthy people could afford not only proud horses to pull their carriages through town, but also expensive bronze models of their vehicles and horses to use in the world of the dead.

The two men became fierce rivals: Xiang Yu, an aristocrat with tradition behind him and powerful allies supporting him, and Liu Bang—a peasant, but one whose mother had dreamed of a god and whose father had seen a dragon, a man who as a boy had saved many people's lives with his bravery, a man whose face was so pleasing that a man would risk his wife's displeasure to have his daughter marry him—and a man with a loyal band of followers who disapproved of the emperor.

The conflict turned into a contest to see who could reach the capital and its great treasures first. The area around the Qin capital would be a special prize because of its riches and historical importance. After its ownership was determined, the rivals would decide who would govern which part of the empire.

Liu entered the region in 207 BCE, before Xiang Yu. He didn't allow any looting or destruction in the capital. According to the *Record of the Historian,* he said to the city's powerful men, "I have come only to save you from injury, not to exploit or oppress you. Therefore do not be afraid!"

Sima Qian, "Basic Annals," *Record of the Historian,* about 100 BCE

He established a new law code. Instead of the complex system established by the Qin, Liu reduced the law to a simple statement: "Those who murder will be killed; those who injure or steal will be punished according to their offenses." Period.

Xiang Yu was far away in the east when Liu made his triumphant entry into the capital. He didn't learn for another year that Liu had beaten him to the Qin region. He was furious and decided to get rid of his rival. Liu had only 100,000 soldiers whereas Xiang had 400,000, so Liu surrendered and turned the capital over to Xiang Yu.

According to the *History of the Han,* Xiang wanted to kill Liu Bang, but he couldn't bring himself to do it. One of his advisers told a warrior named Xiang Zhuang, "Go in and do a sword dance and use this as a pretext to strike and kill the Lord of Pei. Otherwise, all of you are going to become his slaves."

Sima Qian, "Basic Annals," *Record of the Historian,* about 100 BCE

Xiang Zhuang asked Liu Bang for permission to perform a sword dance for him. One of Liu's followers was suspicious about this, so he "also rose and danced, always using his body to shield the Lord of Pei." Once the dance was over, Liu Bang excused himself, saying he had to go to the

Ban Gu, *History of the Han*, first century CE

bathroom, and then, as the *History of the Han* says, "Leaving behind carriage and officials, he fled alone on horseback," leaving Xiang Yu in charge—at least for the time being.

Unlike Liu Bang, who had kept things peaceful when he took over the capital, Xiang Yu burned most of the city to the ground, killing thousands of inhabitants. This couldn't have won him many supporters in the capital. He decided to allow Liu Bang to become King of Han, a region in northern Sichuan province.

Liu was enraged at the double cross. After all, he had been the first to enter the capital, and he should have been ruling it. Instead, his rival had given him a small and far-off kingdom to govern.

SO WHAT'S THE DIFFERENCE?

Recently, archaeologists have found portions of both the Qin and Han legal codes. Comparison of them showed that they were actually quite similar. The basic structure of the government remained the same, and many Qin laws stayed in force. Maybe the prohibition against killing, injuring, and thieving was just a summary of what Liu's laws were intended to prevent, or was supposed to impress people with the directness of his rule. In any case, the simple statement was an effective way to tell his subjects what he thought was important, even if it was too brief to serve as a law code for running an enormous and complicated state.

An 18th-century Chinese painter gave the peasant Liu Bang a royal appearance, foretelling his later rise to emperor. From humble beginnings, Liu Bang would go on to found the Han dynasty.

Liu went on the offensive. His army took control of the whole area around the capital. He went on to capture the state of Chu, Xiang Yu's base of power. Liu had some close calls—in 205 BCE, Xiang almost captured him, and in 204 BCE Xiang challenged him to a duel to settle the whole matter. Liu thought this proposal was outrageous, and he made a long speech denouncing Xiang. "You as a vassal killed your lord," he said, "you killed those who had already surrendered, you governed unjustly, and you led people in taking an oath then did not keep to it. The world has no place for a traitor without principles." He concluded scornfully, "I am leading my righteous troops, in obedience to the various lords, to execute the remaining bandits. I would send a criminal who managed to escape execution to strike you down. Why should I bother to fight a duel with you myself?"

66 Ban Gu, *History of the Han,* first century CE

Now it was Xiang's turn to lose his temper. To be threatened with death at the hands of a condemned criminal! This was too much. He or one of his men shot Liu in the chest with a crossbow. Liu didn't want to let his men know how badly he was hurt, so he sneered, "This slave has hit me in the toe." (Of course Xiang wasn't a slave, but calling him one was a serious insult).

66 Sima Qian, "Basic Annals," *Record of the Historian,* about 100 BCE

Finally, in 203 BCE, Liu's forces outmaneuvered Xiang's army in a battle. Xiang decided to go down fighting. According to the *Record of the Historian,* written about 100 years later, "King Xiang charged, beheading one officer and killing almost a hundred men; when he reassembled his cavalrymen, he had lost only two of them." He plunged into battle again and again. When he realized he was cornered, he said to a Han cavalry officer, "Aren't you an old acquaintance of mine?" The officer took a good look at him, and then called to another officer, "Here is King Xiang!"

66 Sima Qian, "Basic Annals," *Record of the Historian,* about 100 BCE

"I hear," the king said coolly, "that Liu Bang, the leader of the Han, has put a price on my head of a thousand gold pieces and a town with ten thousand homes. I'll do you a favor." And he cut his own throat.

Liu Bang was now emperor. He made a new capital called Chang'an, or Everlasting Peace, and poured money

THE PEOPLE OF THE HAN

Even today the Chinese people call themselves "people of the Han" (*Hanren*) and refer to their language as "the Han language."

A bureaucracy is a large number of officials, usually in a strict rank order. Each official has a specific job. The Chinese had the largest and longest-lasting bureaucracy in history.

into making it the grandest city in the known world. He had a magnificent new palace built. To govern his enormous new empire, he created a **bureaucracy** to manage affairs. He fought off attacks by others who wanted to take over, and battled against foreign tribes.

He never forgot his peasant origins, though. He was scornful of scholars, and once urinated into a scholar's hat (the man wasn't wearing it at the time). It was not only scholars whom he disliked, however. Liu didn't trust merchants, and he didn't approve of military men being in prominent positions in the government.

So who was left to help the new emperor run things? He chose landowners, the people with whom Liu had worked so successfully as leader of his *ting*. Liu began putting men from this class into the government, and families sent him their most capable sons.

Liu Bang was a popular leader. When he passed through his home region of Pei late in his life, children sang songs for him. He told the people that they didn't have to pay taxes, which must have made him even more popular.

Liu was not only a humble peasant who ended up as emperor, but he was the founder of the great Han dynasty. For four centuries after his death, Han emperors worshipped him as their **Gaozu**, or "Lofty Ancestor."

高祖
gao + *zu* = "high," "lofty" + "ancestor"

"*A great wind arises, the clouds are borne aloft,*

Having awed all within the seas, I return to my home.

Where shall I find valiant knights to guard the four quarters?"

—Liu Bang, "Song of the Great Wind," *Shiji*, about 100 BCE

CHAPTER 15

WHO IS CHINESE?
ETHNIC GROUPS AND CHINA

> People belong to the same ethnic group if they share racial, cultural, religious, or language characteristics.

People of different **ethnic groups** have lived in China since prehistoric times. The modern Chinese government says there are 56 different ethnic groups in the country, although some people think that there are actually hundreds. The largest group—the Han, named for the dynasty that ruled China from 206 BCE to 220 CE—makes up about 92 percent of the population.

The early rulers of China didn't divide their neighbors into groups. They didn't even really bother to try to tell them apart. They said that they themselves lived in the center of the world, and referred to the people around them as barbarians of the east (*yi*), barbarians of the west (*rong*), barbarians of the south (*man*), and barbarians of the north (*di*).

The Han rulers pushed China's borders out as far as the plains of Mongolia and the territory of the Xiongnu to the north. They eventually controlled areas that are now Vietnam and Korea, Central Asia up to the Taklamakan Desert, and almost to the area occupied by the country of Myanmar (Burma) today. Many of the huge numbers of people the Han conquered were absorbed into Chinese culture. China began to rely heavily on these new people as a source of wealth (through taxes) and soldiers and slaves.

But some of the groups that joined the Chinese Empire were so different from their rulers that they were a challenge to govern. Some had no fixed home and many didn't have names in the same way that the Chinese did, with a clan name followed by a personal name. Without an address and an easily recognizable name, these people were difficult to keep track of. One solution was to appoint local leaders to run things. Occasionally people would object to being governed by even a local person if he was appointed by the far-away and foreign rulers, and they would rebel, killing the leader.

But generally these revolts weren't too difficult to control. The real problem came from outsiders—either people who

NOT REALLY HUMAN

The names that the Chinese used for these "barbarians" show the contempt they felt for them. Part of the character for the *di* (狄) means dog (犭), and the character for *man* (蠻) has an element that means "insect" or "reptile" 虫.

resisted the Han dynasty's control, or those on the edges of the Han territory. Many of these people lingered nearby, threatening their Chinese neighbors and their possessions.

Some of the groups threatening the borders of the empire were nomads—people without a fixed home, who travel with herd animals. Many nomads of Central Asia also depended on agriculture, so they were partially nomadic, or seminomadic. Central Asia was—and still is—a good location for nomadic tribes because of the number of oases and streams where they could get water. Nomads traded their meat, milk, and hides for cloth and other supplies in small villages in Central Asia.

Life was good in Central Asia, by nomadic standards. Still, it must have irritated the nomads when the Chinese took over land that they had always used for pastureland and small farming. The new Chinese settlements certainly

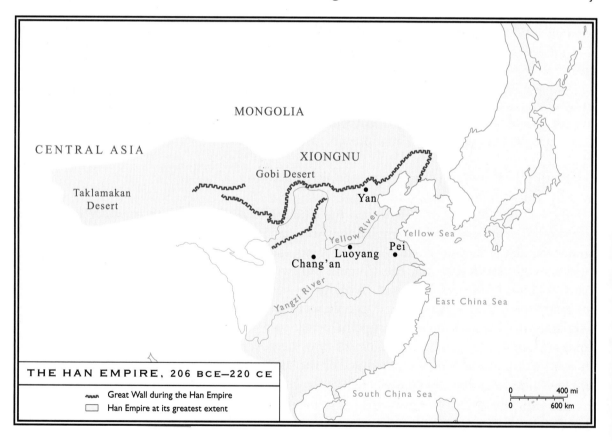

THE HAN EMPIRE, 206 BCE—220 CE

⌇⌇⌇ Great Wall during the Han Empire
☐ Han Empire at its greatest extent

made a tempting target. The Han rulers knew that the many wandering tribes posed a serious threat to their power. They tried to win the allegiance of the nomad rulers in various ways, even giving them women from the imperial family as brides.

The women sent to these distant lands often lived very sad lives, cut off from their relatives and the only life they had ever known. The Chinese rulers thought it was worth it, though, since they hoped to "civilize" the nomads by mixing in Chinese blood with the "barbarian" line. A beautiful woman named Wang Zhaojun was sent to the harem of Emperor Yuan in 39 or 38 BCE, when she was 18 years old, but she refused to pay extra for a beautiful portrait so the court painter made an ugly painting of her. The emperor was put off by it and never visited her. He decided to marry her off to a Xiongnu ruler, and as she was leaving for her new home, the emperor saw her for the first time. He was awestruck by her beauty but could not go back on his word. (He did, however, have the painter executed.) Wang Zhaojun spent the rest of her life among the Xiongnu. Her children were all married to Xiongnu nobles and her sons and grandsons held important positions. A second-century CE poet named Cai Yong wrote a song that he imagined she might have sung on her way to meet her husband, ending:

A Naxi religious leader, called a Dongba, performs a ritual. The Naxi tribespeople from Yunnan and Sichuan provinces in Western China follow an ancient religion that mixes Daoism and their own beliefs.

> The swallow flapping its wings
> Perches among the Western Qiang.
> Lofty mountains tower there,
> The water of the River sparkles.
>
> Oh, father! Oh, mother!
> The road's far and long.
> Alas! I'm forlorn.
> My heart is sore torn.

Invasion by barbarians—or, from another point of view, attempts by nomadic tribes to reclaim lands they had always used—was nothing new. An anonymous poem in a collection called the *Book of Poetry* that was put together in the seventh century BCE expresses the sorrow of soldiers about to leave on a long military campaign:

📖 Cai Yong, *Lute Songs*, late-second century BCE

❝ Anonymous, *Book of Poetry*, seventh century BCE

When shall we return? When shall we return?
It will be late in the [next] year.
Wife and husband will be separated,
Because of the Xianyun [Xiongnu].
We shall have no leisure to rest,
Because of the Xianyun.

In fact, the threat of invasion was so serious that in the seventh century BCE the Chinese began construction on a huge wall to keep out wandering tribes. Different states along the northern border of China each built small barriers until the Qin rulers joined the pieces in the late third century BCE. The Qin then expanded the wall until it was 3,000 miles (5,000 kilometers) long. Huge numbers of laborers worked on this massive project—it took 300,000 workers just to put together the various pieces. The builders used local materials, so in rocky areas they built segments of the wall out of stone and used wood in forested places. In most cases the base of the wall is hard-packed earth.

The Han expanded on the Qin construction. A major challenge was how to build the wall across the vast and forbidding Gobi Desert. One solution was to rely more on ditches and moats than on actual walls in this area. The huge structure is known today as the Great Wall of China.

Building the Great Wall was difficult and dangerous work. Some historians think that the number of people who

Wang Shaojun looks back wistfully as she is forced to leave China. Artists always show her carrying a lute to accompany the sad song she sings as she departs.

In 2003, China's first astronaut, Yang Liwei, told reporters that he could not see the Great Wall from space. But an American astronaut says Yang just wasn't looking in the right place. The American claims that he has seen it from his position in the International Space Station, which is even farther away than Yang's spaceship was when he looked for the wall.

died building the wall was greater than the number of people whose lives were saved by its construction. One estimate is that for every yard of wall, one worker died. An account in the *History of the Han* says,

> Hundreds of thousands of soldiers [working on the wall] were constantly exposed to the elements, and the dead were too numerous to count. Corpses filled the fields and blood flowed a thousand *li* [about 300 miles]. The common people were exhausted and five out of ten homes wanted to rebel.

66 Ban Gu, *History of the Han*, first century CE

The wall was a great achievement. It is so enormous that some people say it's visible from outer space. The wall showed neighboring states that the Chinese were powerful and wealthy. The fact that they had the power and wealth to build such a structure in and of itself must have been intimidating enough to discourage some enemies from attacking.

Was the Great Wall worth the expense, the loss of life, the draining of labor from farming and other productive occupations? To the rulers who ordered the building of the Great Wall, the deaths of many people might have seemed a small price to pay for security.

CHAPTER 16

PRECEPTS FOR WOMEN AND FENG YAN'S LETTER

HARD WORK AND HUMILITY

WOMEN IN ANCIENT CHINA

Ban Zhao, *Precepts for Women,* 80 CE

On the third day after the birth of a girl, our ancestors observed three customs: first, they placed her below the bed; second, they gave her a piece of a broken pot to play with; and third, they made an offering to announce her birth to the gods. Putting the baby below the bed showed that she was lowly and weak,... giving her a potsherd to play with showed that she should work hard,... and announcing her birth to the ancestors clearly meant that she ought to think of her main duty as performing the sacrifices in her home.

The historian Ban Zhao wrote these words describing the customs of the earlier Warring States period (480–221 BCE) to open the first chapter of her *Precepts [Rules] for Women* in about 80 CE. Of all the topics she covered in her book, the three values that she mentions in these opening lines—humility, hard work, and religious observance—were the most important virtues for women in ancient China.

Ban Zhao, *Precepts for Women,* 80 CE

Ban Zhao defines humility, the first trait, as "yielding and acting respectful, putting others first and herself last." If a woman does something well, she shouldn't mention it (although she must have hoped that someone else would bring it up!). She should "even endure [it] when others speak or do evil to her."

Women in ancient China had a lot of practice in humility. They were considered inferior to men in just about every way. In their culture a man's job was to control women and a woman's job was to serve men. If they didn't do this, Ban Zhao says, "then the proper relationship between men and women and the natural order of things are neglected and destroyed."

Ban Zhao, *Precepts for Women,* 80 CE

Parents usually didn't think it was worth investing much in their daughters, either financially or emotionally, because someday a girl would leave and become a member of another family. All the hard work and expense of raising a daughter would benefit her husband's family. Of course, a properly brought-up girl would be easier to marry off. This meant that daughters weren't completely abandoned, and the way a wife behaved would bring either pride or disgrace to her parents and the rest of her birth family. Ban Zhao worried about this in her own case, saying, "I constantly feared that I would disgrace myself, thereby increasing the shame of my parents."

Because wives became members of their husbands' families, not their birth families, most people wanted sons much more than they wanted daughters. Daughters were only temporary members of the family, and they were an expense to raise. Some sources say that after a three-day-old baby girl was left beneath the bed, the family could choose whether or not to pick her up. If they didn't, she would be left to die unless someone else saved her, perhaps to serve as a slave. That way the family could concentrate its energy and resources on other (especially male) children.

After humility, the next virtue that Ban Zhao mentioned was hard work. Most women in ancient China did work very hard. Many tasks involved in farming—plowing a field, weeding, transporting heavy buckets of water—were difficult, and everyone in a farming family worked every day. Women also did the weaving that provided clothing, and if they were skilled enough, they could sell excess cloth. Some women made straw sandals to sell. All women prepared and served food, except in the few families wealthy enough to afford slaves or paid servants.

Few jobs that women could hold paid well enough to make them rich. On rare occasions, a woman was able to set up shop selling handcrafts or other goods. One widow inherited her husband's **cinnabar** mines and ran them skillfully enough to become one of the wealthiest merchants in

This terracotta figurine from the Han dynasty shows the style of dress and hair popular during the Han.

Cinnabar is a reddish mineral used as a dye.

A shaman is someone thought to be able to communicate with and influence the spirit world. Shamans are often priest-doctors.

❝ Ban Zhao, *Precepts for Women,* 80 CE

DIVORCE, ANCIENT CHINESE STYLE

The seven reasons for which a husband could get a divorce were his wife's fighting with his parents, her inability to have children, adultery, jealousy, incurable disease, talking too much, and theft. Women could divorce their husbands—it's not known on what grounds—during the Han dynasty (202 BCE to 220 CE) and perhaps at other times as well.

❝ Feng Yan, letter, 60 CE

China in the first century CE. Entertainers, such as singers and dancers, usually didn't earn much money, although some might become popular and gain wealth and power if their admirers were influential. If a **shaman** did good work, she could earn a decent living.

A few women, especially the daughters of scholars, were educated. Ban Zhao, who received her learning at home from her mother, thought that education for some girls was a good idea: "It is the rule to begin to teach children to read at the age of eight years. By the age of fifteen years they ought then to be ready for cultural training. Only why should it not be that girls' education as well as boys' be according to this principle?"

Some women received enough schooling to became physicians (treating only female patients), but they never could be teachers or politicians. Women were not allowed to act and talk freely around men, so it would be impossible for them to be effective in a classroom or a political office.

Ban Zhao's third value, after humility and hard work, was religious observance. Not much is known about what women did to uphold the religious traditions of their home. In modern China, women are primarily responsible for making family offerings to the gods and ancestors, and some historians think that this was probably the case in ancient China as well.

People got married for many reasons, mostly economic. Of course many married couples loved each other, but affection was just an added bonus. One old man named Feng Yan apparently had a hard time even living in the same house as his wife. He wrote a letter to her brother in about 60 CE, saying that although "man is a creature of emotion, . . . it is according to reason [and not emotion] that husband and wife are put together." He evidently regrets whatever reason it was that led him to marry his wife and to stay with her, saying that his "wife is jealous and has destroyed the Way of a good family. Yet this mother of five children is still in my house." He complains that she bosses him around, can't take a joke, and nags him about his eating habits, saying, "if I eat too much or too little, or if I drink too much or

Ban Zhao, also known as Madame Cao, tutors the empress and other ladies in the court. She is considered the first female historian in China.

too little, she jumps all over me." She's lazy: "When she is at home, she is always lounging in bed. After she gave birth to my principal heir, she refused to have any more children."

She scolds him, Feng Yan claims, mistreats their servant, doesn't do the laundry, and leaves the house looking like a pigsty. She enlists the aid of a local official to help her get what she wants and doesn't listen to her own relatives when they try to reason with her.

Feng Yan decided that he was finally going to get rid of her, declaring:

> Unless I send this wife back, my family will have no peace. Unless I send this wife back, my house will never be clean. Unless I send this wife back, good fortune will not come to my family. Unless I send this wife back, I will never again get anything accomplished.

66 *Feng Yan, letter, 60* CE

A DANCING EMPRESS

One dancer even became empress. Her name, Zhao Feiyan, means Flying Swallow and may have been made up for use on the stage. After she caught the emperor's eye, she became his concubine. She accused the empress of black magic, and then became the emperor's official wife and empress herself.

❝ Ban Zhao, *Precepts for Women,* 80 CE

and he concludes sadly, "I hate myself for not having made this decision while I was still young."

It would be interesting to hear his wife's side of the story. She might have seen things much differently. Feng Yan says, for example, that he didn't send her back to her birth family earlier because he didn't want his children to have to take on heavy household labor. This seems to imply that she actually did work, or else why would her leaving have made them work harder? Maybe the house was a mess *despite* her efforts to keep it clean.

Rule books such as *Precepts for Women* are an interesting way to find out how people thought others should behave. But if everyone did things correctly all the time, there would be no need to tell them how to act. The mere existence of Ban Zhao's book tells us that some women needed to be reminded how to behave, and Feng Yan's letter shows us that at least one of them didn't seem to care about the rules.

Obviously, Feng Yan's wife didn't just hang around at home, as a virtuous woman was supposed to do. How could she go running to the local magistrate and get him on her side if she did? Just as obviously, she was talking to unrelated men—if the magistrate who took her side had been her brother or uncle, Feng Yan would have been sure to point this out, so he must not have been a relative. Both of these behaviors would have shocked Ban Zhao and others concerned with women's proper actions.

Ban Zhao says that a virtuous woman must "choose her words with care, avoid vulgar language, speak at appropriate times, and not weary others with much conversation." Of course, we have only Feng Yan's view of his wife's conversational style, but according to him, when a family member tries to reason with her, "she flings insults at them and makes sharp retorts."

Not only the family members felt the force of her words. Her husband says that if he "plays some affectionate joke on her, she will gossip about it with everyone." (Sometimes people disagree about what is an affectionate joke and the wife might not have seen the humor in whatever it was that Feng did.) Her gossip and complaints were so convincing that Feng thought that the neighbors believed what she said and disapproved of him, making him feel "as if there were a hundred crossbows around our house."

If you set these two documents side by side and compare what they say, it appears that the only way a woman could have any influence or make her opinion known would be to break all the rules and become as disagreeable as possible. That's a problem with drawing big conclusions based on very little evidence, like these two documents. It's very likely that most women may have treated their husbands and neighbors with respect and were also treated that way themselves, and still had some power in their own lives. Until an archaeologist turns up another letter or document praising a virtuous woman who also had the ability to control at least part of her own life, all we have are documents such as Ban Zhao's rules, and the description of a woman whose husband claimed she broke all of them.

" Feng Yan, letter, 60 CE

In the legend retold in this print, a woman named Meng Jiangnü went in search of her husband, a worker on the Great Wall. She discovered that he had died and was buried in the wall. Her wail of grief made the wall crack, revealing his bones, which she could then bring home for a decent burial.

CHAPTER 17

❝ MOZI, LETTER TO ZHU XI, AND COMPLETE RECORD OF MILITARY MATTERS

NEW WAYS OF DOING THINGS
INVENTIONS AND TECHNOLOGY

Wheelbarrows, kites, paper—everyone is familiar with them. When you think of a wheelbarrow, what comes to mind? Gardening or construction work, most likely. Kites probably make you imagine colorful paper or plastic constructions that you fly on the beach or in an open field. And paper is so common that most people hardly think about it, but when they do, it's usually because they're using some for homework or an art project.

But if you were to mention these same items—wheelbarrows, kites, paper—to a person in the Han dynasty of ancient China, that person might assume that you were thinking about warfare.

We're so accustomed to seeing these things used in certain ways that it's difficult to imagine how useful they would be in a military setting. But what is a wheelbarrow, after all? An inexpensive wheeled vehicle that can be powered by a single person to

Ancient Chinese people can be credited with many useful inventions, including the wheelbarrow. They also wrote about their inventions so that others could re-create them. This illustration of a merchant transporting his goods comes from a 17th-century book on technology called The Lord of Heaven Invents Things.

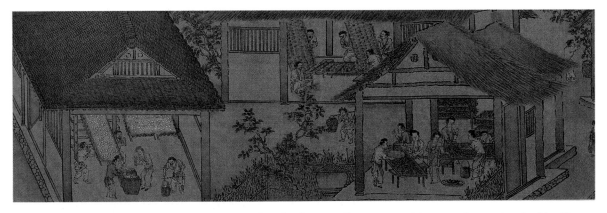

move heavy things over uneven ground. The huge Chinese armies were constantly in need of food, clothing, medical equipment, and ammunition. Wheelbarrows were an efficient way to carry heavy and bulky supplies (and even people) over land that was often too rocky and mountainous for larger wheeled vehicles. The first images of these useful vehicles appeared in Chinese tomb decorations around 100 CE, but they had probably been in use since at least the first century BCE.

An ancient Chinese wheelbarrow wasn't always a simple cart with handles and a single wheel in front. There were many variations in their construction, especially in the size and placement of the wheels, which could be large or small, and which could rely on one central wheel in front or in the center. The Chinese adapted the form for different terrains. One ingenious inventor even thought of manufacturing wheelbarrows with sails attached. They could reach speeds of up to 40 miles per hour over land or ice.

Kites are so fragile that their military use would be limited today. But when you realize that kites were the first heavier-than-air aircraft known to the world, possibilities begin to open up. Kites may have been used to help far-flung soldiers communicate in a battle. A combination of colors and shapes of kites could serve as a code to send a message. The *Mozi* says that a general "constructed a bird from bamboo and wood and when it was completed he flew it. It stayed up for three days." Although nobody knows exactly how the kites were used, it's unlikely that these serious

Many people were involved in silk production. In small, home-based workshops, women were often important in sericulture (the making of silk). In this picture, women feed the worms on the right, while men on the left sort the cocoons.

[66] Mozi, *Mozi*, about 400 BCE

FIBER: GOOD FOR DIETS AND PAPER

Paper is made of dissolved cellulose (plant fiber, like the strings in celery) that has been dried in a flat sheet. To make paper, the Chinese would mash or chop up fibrous plants or rags and soak or boil them in a solution to loosen the fibers from the rest of the plant structure. They would fish out the fibers and mix them with something such as flour to make them hold together, and then spread them on a screen or press them into a mold.

Lu You, a letter to Zhu Xi, about 1200 CE

Mao Yuanyi, *Complete Record of Military Matters,* about 1625 CE

warriors were just passing the time between battles. They must have had some warlike function in mind.

Materials for making kites were available in China. Silk is light and strong, and it was ideal for both the fabric of the kite's body and the string that tethered it. Bamboo, which grows in China, is a wood that is light and strong as well as flexible, making it perfect to form a kite's structure.

Today, many people make kites out of paper, which was invented in China by at least the second century BCE. The ancient Chinese used paper in many of the same ways we use it today: for kites, for writing and painting, as toilet paper, as wallpaper, for blowing noses. But would you believe armor was made of paper?

In the 1960s there was a brief fad for paper clothing in much of the United States and Europe. The people who wore these throwaway clothes might have been surprised to learn that the Chinese people of long ago used paper clothing. It wasn't disposable, like the more modern version, and in fact its owners prized it for its warmth and softness. Many centuries later, a poet praised a paper blanket, saying, "It is whiter than fox fur and softer than cotton." Multiple layers of paper can be extremely tough, too—just try to poke a hole in a phone book if you don't believe that. Eventually, Chinese soldiers wore armor made of pleated paper. They valued it because it was strong and light as well as protective. The Chinese used paper armor for hundreds of years. In about 1625, Mao Yuanyi said, "The best choice for foot soldiers is paper armor, mixed with a variety of silk and cloth."

These inventions and others spread through Asia and eventually throughout the world. Some were thought of independently in other parts of the world as well, often long after a Chinese inventor came up with them. Many of these inventions reached other lands through traders. Travel on China's many rivers was a relatively inexpensive and rapid way to trade goods. Whoever had the fastest, strongest, most reliable means of shipping could earn a lot of money, so inventors had an incentive to come up with ways to improve ships.

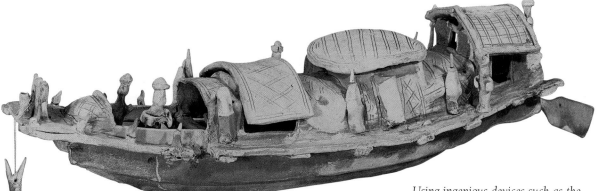

Using ingenious devices such as the rudder to steer the boat accurately, the Chinese sailed far away from their home. They went around the southern tip of Africa and some scholars think they even went as far as North or South America.

Getting your ship headed in the right direction was always a challenge. Early boats had no mechanism for steering. If you can't steer, you have to either wait for the river current and the wind to go the way you want or find a way to work against these forces. Oarsmen can steer by rowing harder and faster on one side than the other, but this uses a lot of energy that could otherwise be channeled into making the boat go forward. A model boat made of pottery, found in a tomb from the first century CE, shows a great innovation: a rudder, which would make steering much easier and would conserve energy.

The position of the sails also makes a difference in the boat's speed and handling. If the sails are fixed in a forward-facing position, the boat can go only in the direction the wind is blowing. But something important changes when sails are placed along the length of the boat, and the bottom of the boat comes down into a ridge. Then the force of the wind against the sail can push the boat forward, even when the wind isn't blowing in the same direction that the boat needs to go. The Chinese pioneered this arrangement, known as fore-and-aft rigging, by at least the second century CE. By the third century CE, a text mentions four-masted boats rigged fore and aft.

It would seem logical to mention the early Chinese invention of the compass here, since today the most common use of this instrument is in navigation. But as it turns out, although the Chinese did find compasses helpful for

OR MAYBE THERE WAS A LOT OF RAIN THAT WEEK?

People sometimes used omens to make a political point. In 185 CE devastating floods left thousands of people homeless. Ancient scholars argued that floods were a *yin* (female) force and they occurred because an empress was running the state.

contrast, according to Wang, poor families had to struggle just to make ends meet. He is quoted in the *History of the Han* as saying,

Ban Gu, *History of the Han*, first century CE

Fathers and sons, husbands and wives plow and weed the entire year, yet what they get is not enough to survive on. That is why the rich, whose dogs and horses have an abundance of beans and grain, commit evil out of pride. The poor, who cannot get their fill living on bran and husks, commit venal crimes out of poverty.

Wang Mang was a follower of the great teacher Confucius, who had lived 500 years earlier. Confucians said that government existed for the people, not the other way around. To a Confucian, the way China was ruled in the first century BCE seemed unjust.

As an outsider living on his relatives' charity, Wang must have been one of the few people of the privileged class to empathize with the underdog. Because he thought he would never be able to make a name for himself as a politician, he became a scholar and worked very hard at his studies. He impressed influential people around him with his intelligence and his good behavior. The *History of the Han* says that he "acted with reverence and humility. He received instruction in the **Classics of Rites**. . . . He labored his body and studied broadly, and wore his robes like a scholar." Not only was he studious and hard working, he also was a dutiful man: "He waited upon his mother and widowed sister-in-law, and raised the orphaned son of his elder brother. His conduct was quite perfect."

Classic (or *Classics*) *of Rites* is a set of three books put together during the Han dynasty that describe the rituals of the earlier Zhou dynasty.

Ban Gu, *History of the Han*, first century CE

Wang wasn't the only person of talent and intelligence who was forced to sit on the sidelines and watch other people make decisions. Only a very few people, in fact, could participate in the government, and almost always those powerful few were from important families or had unusual talents.

One large group of people in ancient China was powerless outside the home, no matter how important their family or how great their abilities. These excluded people were the women. A few women managed to find a way to gain some power, among them some of Wang Mang's relatives. Many empresses of the Han dynasty came from the Wang family. Although empresses supposedly had very little real power themselves, often these wives, and eventually mothers, of emperors exerted some control over policies and laws through the men in charge.

Wang Mang, being a man from an important family, had more of an opportunity to work his way into the government. His first move was to get on the good side of his Uncle Feng, the head of the army, who had fallen ill. The History of the Han says that "Mang waited upon him in his illness. He personally tasted [his uncle's] medicine.... When Feng was about to die, he commended Mang to the empress **dowager** and the emperor." Wang Mang received his first title—Gentleman of the Palace Gate (an attendant of the emperor)—and began his rapid rise to power. His education and talents brought him to the notice of Emperor Cheng and other influential men, and he quickly acquired new titles and responsibilities.

A dowager is the widow of an important man who keeps her late husband's title and often some of his privileges. Dowager empresses often held considerable power in Chinese courts.

Ban Gu, History of the Han, first century CE

Then Wang Mang's ambition received a serious setback. When Emperor Cheng died and a new emperor came to power, Wang Mang proposed that Cheng's mother should remain the most important woman in the court (the fact that she was also Wang's aunt might have had something to do with his insistence). But the new emperor's mother and aunt won out. Some of Wang Mang's enemies took advantage of his humiliating loss and said he should be stripped of his titles and land. The emperor was more compassionate, saying, according to the History of the Han, "Because Mang is related to the Grand Empress Dowager, let him not be removed from his titles, but he is sent to his estate." Wang Mang had to leave the court. It looked as if his chances for more advancement were over.

Ban Gu, History of the Han, first century CE

After five years, the new emperor died and Wang Mang's aunt managed to regain her influence in the court. She called on Wang Mang to take over as commander in chief, and together they put a nine-year-old boy on the throne. But actually it was Wang Mang, not the boy-emperor, who was calling the shots. He had the former emperor's

Today China is the world's largest producer of pigs. Pigs have always been an important source of meat in China (the Chinese word for "meat" also means "pork"). This model of a pigsty was placed in a tomb so that its occupant could feast on pork in the next world.

Ban Gu, History of the Han, first century CE

relatives convicted of crimes and removed from power, giving him free rein to run things.

Despite all his forceful deeds Wang described himself as shy. The History of the Han reports that in 5 CE he confessed in a speech, "When I meet the nobles of the land and have to speak in front of them, I never fail to start sweating out of embarrassment." He explained that this embarrassment arose from a sense of inferiority: "Though I am by nature stupid and vulgar, I know that my virtue is slight but my position is honorable, my ability is weak but my responsibilities are large."

He was probably just being modest, though, because his actions showed him to be anything but awkward and stupid. He became prime minister in 4 CE and made his position even more secure when he had his daughter marry the emperor and become the empress.

In 6 CE the emperor died (there were rumors that Wang Mang had poisoned him), and Wang and his aunt put a two-year-old boy on the throne. Immediately, according to the *History of the Han,* "a white stone [appeared]...with red writing...saying, 'This announces to Mang, Duke Giving Repose to the Han, that he should become emperor.'" More signs appeared, all of them saying that he should be the next emperor.

Ban Gu, *History of the Han,* first century CE

Finally in 9 CE, Wang Mang took the throne as the first emperor of the **Xin** dynasty. He made sure that his influential grandmother stayed on his side by declaring her Empress Dowager of the entire dynasty.

新

Xin = "new"
The name of the Xin dynasty probably refers to Wang's land in Xindu, or "new town."

The description of Wang in the *History of the Han* reflects the respect that people had for their new leader—and also how much they feared him. He "had a large mouth and a receding chin, bulging eyes with fiery pupils, and a loud, hoarse voice. He was five foot seven." He also had a sense of style, and chose clothes that made himself look even more imposing. "He was fond of thick shoes and tall hats. He wore padded clothes and puffed out his chest, and liked to look down on others from on high."

Ban Gu, *History of the Han,* first century CE

Ban Gu, *History of the Han,* first century CE

Wang had been an enthusiastic scholar, and as emperor he continued to further the study of science. Once he had the body of an enemy dissected, probably as a sign of disrespect, but also in the spirit of scientific inquiry. The *History of the Han* says:

> Mang sent the Grand Physician, the Master of Prescriptions, and a skilled butcher to dissect and flay him. They weighed and measured his five organs and used...bamboo to trace out his veins so that they would know where each began and ended, saying that thereby they could cure illness.

Ban Gu, *History of the Han,* first century CE

During his reign, Wang enacted many reforms. Some of them reflect his empathy with the lower classes, and others show his desire to return to a way of life from a thousand years earlier. Among his reforms were:

- abolishing the slave trade (nobody knows when slavery began in China, but by the earlier Han dynasty forced labor was common)

HOW OLD IS THE BABY?

Chinese children are considered one year old when they are born. They turn two at the next New Year. This means that a child born on the last day of the year would be called a two-year-old the next day.

FEROCIOUS MAKEUP

The Red Eyebrows dyed
their eyebrows with
cinnabar, a reddish metal.
The color stands for the
Han dynasty. These peas-
ants from the east made up
the first recorded Chinese
popular religious sect. They
traveled together—women,
men, and children—and
advocated the return of
the Han.

- claiming mountains, forests, streams, and marshes as state property; now the state owned all the natural resources
- reviving laws that limited the rights of merchants, because the Chinese thought they made no real contribution to society
- reestablishing former ranks and titles in an attempt to re-create the social structure of a past era
- establishing a national bank with fair rates of interest
- standardizing currency so that the same coins could be used over the entire nation

Some people were thrilled with the changes Wang made. But those who had prospered under the old way of life were less than enthusiastic, and soon new signs and omens began to appear, but this time they said that Wang should *not* be emperor.

Some groups rebelled against Wang's rule, among them a ferocious band called the Red Eyebrows. Wang was afraid of these human rebels, but he was also concerned about the vengeful spirits of the Han dynasty, which had ruled before him. At one point he ordered his soldiers to enter a temple of the founder of the Han dynasty and "draw their swords, throw and strike in all directions, destroy its doors and windows with axes, whip the walls of the building with ochre-red whips and sprinkle them with peach water." He hoped

The square holes in the middle of these coins made it possible for them to be tied together with thread in groups of 1,000, which was a common unit of payment.

Acrobatics were and still are a popular form of entertainment in China. An acrobatics spectacle includes so much activity that the Chinese call it "the hundred sports." This model was made so that the acrobats could perform for the dead person in his tomb.

that this would drive away the spirits that he felt were against him.

Earthly forces turned out to be more of a threat than the spirits of the Han ancestors, however. The Red Eyebrows grew bold enough to kill some government officials. The country was already in dire shape due to a severe famine. The *History of the Han* reports that "people ate each other." People became desperate, and other groups joined with the Red Eyebrows and attacked the capital city.

Wang Mang, equally desperate, freed state prisoners on condition that they become soldiers and join his side. But it was too late. Somebody opened the gates, and rebels flooded in. Wang Mang was hiding in a tower, and an enemy soldier "recognized Mang and cut off his head. Army soldiers tore Mang's body apart limb from limb and cut him into a thousand pieces. Dozens died fighting over parts of his body." Wang's good luck had run out, and his short-lived dynasty came to an end with the reestablishment of the Han.

Emperor Liu Xiu ascended the throne in 25 CE. He set up a new capital in a new city and declared that the Han were in control again. His government did away with most of Wang Mang's reforms, but later generations were to look to them for inspiration.

66 Ban Gu, *History of the Han*, first century CE

66 Ban Gu, *History of the Han*, first century CE

" BIOGRAPHIES OF
DIVINE IMMORTALS,
DEMON ORDINANCES
OF LADY BLUE, AND
COMMANDS AND
ADMONITIONS FOR
THE FAMILIES OF THE
GREAT DAO

CHAPTER 19

A NEW RELATIONSHIP WITH THE GODS
THE RISE OF DAOISM

GREAT PEACE

Commands and Admonitions for the Families of the Great Dao, written in 255 CE, expresses many Daoist ideas. One is that everything has an opposite: "If you wish morning, you must first have evening. If you desire Great Peace, you must first experience chaos." The idea that universal peace will follow a period of great upheaval exists in many religions.

" Ge Hong, *Biographies of Divine Immortals,* early fourth century CE

You probably won't ever be faced with this problem, but how would you feel if a god appeared to you and told you to start a new religion?

A man named Zhang Ling, who had left his native Jiangsu in eastern China in search of gods and divine secrets, said this happened to him. His wanderings took him clear across the country to the western province of Sichuan in 142 CE. At the top of Cranecall Mountain, Zhang Ling was treated to the sight of the great teacher Laozi, the legendary author of a book written centuries earlier about the Dao, the guiding principle of the universe. On the mountaintop Zhang saw Laozi descend from the clouds surrounded by a group of spirits. An account from the *Biographies of Divine Immortals* of the early fourth century CE describes the vision: "Suddenly a Heavenly Man descended, accompanied by a thousand chariots and ten thousand horsemen, in a golden carriage with a feathered canopy. Riding dragons and astride tigers, they were too numerous to count." Zhang later said that Laozi told him of a new relationship between humans and the gods, summed up in the simple sentence: "The gods do not eat or drink."

This might not seem like such a big deal. After all, if the sacrifices that people had performed for all those centuries turned out to be a waste of time, all they had to do was say, "Sorry, we won't do that anymore" and then go about their business—right?

Wrong. This statement says more than just that these new gods didn't consume sacrificial food, although that was certainly part of it. First, it means that the gods described by Laozi were not physical at all, since they had no need of meat or drink. They were purely spiritual. This was a big change from the idea of divinity that had existed until then,

The Officer of Water was one of the three earliest gods in the Daoist religion. Daoists confessed sins to him and begged for forgiveness once a year.

that the gods shared many characteristics with humans, like hunger, and that they enjoyed the food that people sacrificed to them. Second, it meant that people shouldn't try to bribe the new gods. Bribes didn't work with them, and it was almost an insult to think that their favor could be purchased with a pork chop.

The major ruling principle of the universe, according to the followers of Zhang Ling, was the Dao. This is the same "Dao" (also spelled "Tao") that Laozi had identified in the fourth century BCE as the prime mover of the universe, although his Daoism was different from Zhang Ling's Daoism. For Laozi, the Dao defined a way of living in the world. For Zhang Ling, on the other hand, Daoism was a way to serve the gods. Whether you're talking about Laozi or Zhang Ling, the word "Dao" is hard to define. It is usually translated as "the Way" in English.

The highest Daoist deities are the Three Celestial Worthies. They're not really separate from the Dao, but are its **qi**, or breaths. Below them is another group of three gods, known as the Officers of Heaven, Earth, and Water. They are much more involved in daily life than the Three Celestial Worthies. The Officers watch everybody and record what

氣

qi = "breath" or "ether"
Qi is the air you breathe, but also your energy or vitality.

they do. Early Daoists wrote out three confessions when they committed a wrong, one to each officer, asking forgiveness and promising not to repeat the bad action.

After Zhang Ling received his vision of Laozi and the statement that the gods do not eat or drink, he became a kind of holy man. According to the *Biographies of Divine Immortals*, he was able to cure illness and "commoners flocked to serve him as their teacher. His disciples came to number several tens of thousands of households." This popularity became too much for him to handle on his own, so "he therefore established Libationers [priests] to divide up and take charge of the households." He was honored with the addition of the word "Dao" to his name, giving him the new name of Zhang Daoling, and the title Celestial Master. But it was his grandson Zhang Lu who was really responsible for spreading the religion.

Under Zhang Lu, Daoism became more than a religion alone. He created a state, which he governed under Daoist ideals from around 180 to 215 CE. Every member of the state over the age of seven—including females, which was a revolutionary idea—was a priest in one way or another. Everyone could call on spirit generals—repentant demons who led armies of fallen soldiers against bad spirits—for help. Only the followers of the Dao would be among the "seed people" who would survive the disasters the followers thought were approaching. The seed people would repopulate the world, like seeds planted in a field, in the paradise that would follow, called Great Peace. A book with the mysterious title, *Demon Ordinances of Lady Blue*, from around the fourth century CE says that the Dao itself spoke through a medium to say, "The Masters of the

66 Ge Hong, *Biographies of Divine Immortals*, early fourth century CE

Daoists adopted the traditional Chinese goddess known as the Queen Mother of the West and turned her into a goddess who reveals secrets to the worthy. The goddess's servant carries the peaches of immortality that grow only every 3,000 years at the Queen Mother's palace.

This manuscript from the early sixth century CE records Zhang Lu's explanation of how his followers should understand the Daodejing.

Three Offices will select the seed people and take...eighteen thousand in number. How many have there been up until today? The great quota is not yet full."

Daoism was more than a religion. It was a way of life in which the members worked together to build roads, repair bridges, and perform other works for the common good. For instance, they set up charity houses to feed hungry people and they allowed the local non-Chinese people, the Ba, to become full members of the region.

The religion founded by Zhang Daoling and his descendants has changed in the 2,000 years since its beginning, but the basics remain the same. Today most Daoists trace their religion back to the one founded by Zhang Daoling and they still worship the Daoist gods. The 64th Celestial Master, who claims Zhang Daoling as his ancestor, lives in Taiwan today. And the Daoists are still waiting for Great Peace.

❝ Anonymous, *Demon Ordinances of Lady Blue*, about fourth century CE

FIERCE SUPPORTERS

China was, and is, made up of many different ethnic groups. Native peoples called the Ba lived in the eastern part of Sichuan province. They were fierce warriors and were famous for their dances with weapons, which they often performed at the imperial court. Many Ba became devout Daoists and were an important source of support for the new religion. One hundred years after Zhang Ling established his Daoist state, a Ba leader tried unsuccessfully to create a Daoist kingdom in Sichuan.

CHAPTER 20

"A GOLDEN MAN"
BUDDHISM AND THE SILK ROAD

❝ Fan Ye, *Book of the Later Han,*
445 CE

In a dream Emperor Ming saw a golden man, great and tall, the nape of his neck aglow. When he questioned his assembled ministers about him, one of them said, "In the east there is a god, whose name is Fo, a rod six feet [about 12 feet or 4 meters] in height and golden in color."

Intrigued, the emperor sent a messenger to the West to find out about this god—or at any rate, that's the story as reported in the *Book of the Later Han* written by Fan Ye in 445 CE. Later scholars thought that the golden man of the dream must have been the Buddha, a holy man of India, whose religion had been known in China for several decades by Emperor Ming's time (he ruled from 58 to 75 CE).

The Buddha (this title means "enlightened one" in the ancient Indian language of Sanskrit) was an Indian prince named Siddhartha Gautama who lived about 500 years before Emperor Ming. His overprotective father kept him closed up in the palace to shield him from the world's harshness. Siddhartha was curious about what was going on outside the palace walls, so he sneaked out of the palace grounds and went in search of the daily life of ordinary people. For the first time the sheltered prince saw poverty, physical suffering, and

Chinese artists studied the works of artists from other lands. This figure of the Buddha, although made in China, looks much more like statues made in India, the Buddha's homeland, and his face looks more Indian than Chinese.

death. Shocked, he went farther out into the world, searching for truth and understanding. While meditating under a tree, he reached what he called the Four Noble Truths:

1. All existence is suffering.
2. Suffering is caused by wanting things.
3. Therefore, if you don't want anything, you won't suffer.
4. You can stop wanting things if you keep to the right path in eight ways: by having the right view, thought, speech, behavior, means of earning a living, effort, mindfulness, and concentration.

The Buddha said that if people are tied to wanting things, they won't be able to leave the world even when they die. They'll get reborn again and again until they finally manage to stop craving material objects. Then the cycle of rebirth will be broken, and they will enter Nirvana, where individual personality is lost and merges with the Eternal: the unchanging, everlasting part of the universe.

Buddhism spread throughout South Asia, but it took a while for it to arrive in China. A lot of obstacles stood in the way. First, there was a formidable physical barrier: the Taklamakan Desert between the two areas is so harsh that locals still call it the "Land of Death." It has very few oases and its high winds produce many sandstorms. And once you've made it out of the desert, things don't improve too

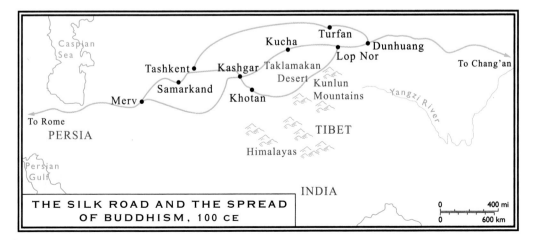

THE SILK ROAD AND THE SPREAD OF BUDDHISM, 100 CE

THE SILK PEOPLE

Some scholars think that Roman soldiers first saw silk in the hands of the Parthians, people who lived in what is now northeastern Iran. The Parthians told the Romans that they had gotten it from mysterious people in the East, whom the Romans then called the Seres: silk people. The Parthians took on the role of middlemen between the Romans and the Chinese, buying silk and then selling it at a profit.

❝ Ban Gu, *History of the Han,* first century CE

much—you come to another desert, the Gobi, and some of the highest mountain ranges in the world.

Second, the Chinese and South Asians had such different ways of life and such different languages that even once they encountered one another, they had a great deal of difficulty communicating.

Third, even if there had been a road, and even if the mountains and desert hadn't stood in the way, it was a long, long distance to travel.

But just like Prince Siddhartha, the people of China weren't content to remain inside their homes. Like him, they were curious. And they had another motivation for travel—trade. At the time that Buddhism was spreading through Asia, in the late-first century BCE, Chinese silk appeared in Rome.

How did it get there? It probably didn't come directly from China. Most likely Chinese merchants traded silk with someone, who traded it to someone else, who traded it again until it reached Italy. In any case, the Romans were eager for more of the luxurious fabric and for the spices that they imported from Asia. The *History of the Han,* written about 100 CE and quoting a text from 91 BCE, says that at first, trade was mostly in curiosities: the Parthians, people who traded between Asia and Europe, "offered to the Han court large birds' eggs, and [Syrian] jugglers." The Chinese were intrigued by the Westerners, noting that they had ostriches and that they wrote "in rows running sideways" (Chinese writing was in vertical columns).

But both sides soon discovered that even more exciting items were available. Along with silk, the Westerners developed a taste for the ceramics, jade, perfumes, spices, and metal objects made by the skilled Chinese craftspeople. In return, the Chinese wanted wool, gold, silver, ivory, jewels, glass, and foods that were new and exotic to them, such as figs and walnuts, from Western Asia and Europe.

These were all precious items. Traders who could get a caravan-load of these goods to its destination would soon be very wealthy. But so would thieves who intercepted the caravan. As merchants developed different routes around and through the mountains and deserts, bandits waited to attack.

Two-humped Bactrian camels can carry up to 500 pounds at a time and can go for many days without water. Without them, the Chinese would have found it nearly impossible to carry out trade across the shifting sands of the Silk Route.

A merchant captured and sold into slavery after trying to earn a fortune through trade in luxurious items might agree with the Buddha that attachment to material objects brings suffering.

Still, the potential rewards were great, so traders kept working, often with body-guards to protect them. The various routes known as the Silk Road became well traveled—all 4,000 miles of them. Not only did traders move goods, but they also brought new ideas and beliefs, which were examined and rejected or accepted. Among these beliefs was Buddhism. In fact, some of the early Buddhist monks in China were originally merchants, or the sons and grandsons of traders. But unlike a jade sculpture or a gold coin, when an idea is passed along to someone else, it often changes.

Buddhism had entered China by at least the first century CE. At first, most Buddhists lived in the capital and large trading centers (because the traders had brought the religion into the country). But Chinese culture was quite different from the Indian society of Prince Siddhartha's time. Some practices and concepts that Indians could accept very easily were difficult for the Chinese to understand.

For example, Buddhist monks left—and still leave—their families and never married. In Chinese culture, having children was very important. Chinese people showed respect to their parents by having children to carry on their family line. They also showed respect by not harming their parents'

GOOD BEHAVIOR

Most religions have rules that followers are supposed to obey. One example is the Ten Commandments found in the Jewish and Christian Bible. Another is the Five Precepts of Buddhism, which prohibit killing, stealing, sexual misconduct, lying or slander, and drinking alcohol.

gift to them: their own bodies. They were supposed to avoid doing anything to harm themselves, including cutting their hair. Buddhist monks, on the other hand, shaved their heads, and some burned cones of incense on their scalps to prove that they could concentrate even when in pain.

The Chinese saw history in 500-year cycles, which they considered to be very long. The Indians imagined eternity in millions of years.

The soul was an important concept in Buddhism, where the soul is reborn into another body after death. But this was a new concept to the ancient Chinese, who did not accept the idea of an eternal soul. And how can you worship your dead ancestors—a central ritual in Chinese tradition—if they've been reborn? They might be sitting next to you while you were sacrificing to them in Heaven. This was unimaginable.

Most Chinese gods accepted sacrifices, but the Buddha was not a god. In any case there was no sense in sacrificing when the point is to stop wanting material objects. Still, the emperor sacrificed to the Buddha, because this was the traditional way to express reverence and because the Chinese initially did not understand the Buddhist texts very well.

Very few people in either China or India knew both the language of the sacred texts of Buddhism and literary Chinese. This meant that many of the works were translated into another language and then into Chinese—or into two other languages and only then into Chinese. Every time a text is translated some of the original meaning is lost, so confusion and misinterpretations filled the early Buddhist texts in Chinese.

The Chinese Buddhists did manage to find some familiar ideas that helped them to understand and accept the new religion. A document written by a scholar named Xiang Kai and recorded in the *Book of the Later Han* mentions sacrifices dedicated to both a Daoist god and the Buddha. Xiang points out a basic similarity between Buddhist ideals and the Dao: "The Dao is pure and empty; it values non-action. Loving life and hating killing, it reduces desires and eliminates extravagance." He even speculates that the Buddha and the founder of Daoism were the same person:

66 Fan Ye, *Book of the Later Han,* 445 CE

"Some say that Laozi went in among the barbarians and became the Buddha."

This new Buddhism led to many changes in different parts of Buddhist life, including art. In Chinese Buddhism the worship of images is so important that the religion was also known as ***xiang jiao***. The desire for attractive and precious objects of worship led to growth in the arts, and some of the greatest sculpture, architecture, and painting in China come from Buddhist temples.

Buddhism also helped relieve the problems of younger brothers. Monasteries provided an honorable and useful profession for boys who were left without a way to earn a living when their older brothers inherited the family's property and rank. The monasteries gradually became independent of the government and stopped paying taxes. They set up hospitals and organizations to help people in need, rescuing orphans and providing for homeless people. Some monasteries even came to serve as banks.

Even people's daily lives changed when they became Buddhists. The new ideas of reincarnation and **karma** influenced their behavior, as did tales of terrifying hells reserved for people who behaved badly.

Buddhism as practiced in China spread throughout East Asia and remains an important world religion. It has continued to change and grow through the millennia and to influence the private and public lives of billions of people in China and around the world.

Siddhartha was shocked at the suffering he saw when he sneaked out of his palace. When he saw the serenity and contentment of a monk, he was convinced that the only way to escape pain was through a life devoted to religion.

像教

xiang + jiao = "image" + "teaching," "religion" Eventually, all Chinese religions adopted the use of images of gods.

Karma is the overall sum of the good and bad deeds that you perform, which determines whether you will be punished or rewarded in your next life.

CHAPTER 21

"SOMEONE WITH THE TALENT TO COMMAND"
A GENERAL TAKES CHARGE

MENTION CAO CAO...

Sometimes when you're talking about someone, that person unexpectedly shows up. You might say, "Well, speak of the devil!"—a saying that refers back to an old superstition that if you talk about the devil, he appears. The Chinese equivalent is "Mention Cao Cao and there he is!"

" Chen Shou, *Record of the Three Kingdoms*, 297 CE

Sometimes when people try to hold on to their power, they wind up doing things that actually make them lose it. In 189 CE the Chinese prime minister decided that a group of court officials was becoming too powerful, so he invited a general to come and kill them all. When the officials found out about this plan, they proved that the prime minister was right about their power: they rose up against him, and the whole court—prime minister, emperor, wives, and all—was forced to flee from the capital and leave it empty for seven years.

More trouble was brewing against the government from a rebel group called the Yellow Turbans. They wore yellow scarves around their heads that symbolized their hope for a new power called Yellow Heaven. This Yellow Heaven, they thought, would be the new ruling force of the universe. The Yellow Turbans were causing problems, staking out their own territory in the east and killing government officials there. The general who finally defeated them had started his military career at a low level, but he quickly rose through the ranks. His name was Cao Cao.

Cao Cao had shown promise of leadership from an early age. A wise man told him, according to his biography in the late third century CE *Record of the Three Kingdoms*, "The empire is falling into disorder and only someone with the talent to command the age can save it. It is up to you to secure the empire!"

Through his military prowess, connections, intelligence, and talent, Cao Cao gained so much power that eventually even the emperor did what he said. He was a great general, and a poet as well. In his *Essay on the Classics* (written about 220 CE), his son Cao Pi said,

This illustration from a novel about the Three Kingdoms shows Liu Bei leading his army to victory. This picture helped people who had never been in a war imagine what it was like.

My father's elegant pursuit was poetry and literature. Even when he was on campaign, he always had a book in his hand. He was always concentrating on his reading as if he had no other concern. He often said, "When a person is young and fond of learning, then his mind is concentrated; as he grows older, he becomes forgetful."

66 Cao Pi, *Essay on the Classics,* about 220 CE

Although he was a soldier, Cao Cao didn't love war, as he shows in a poem about the devastation that conflict leaves in its wake:

Men start arguing over advantageous positions
And soon they're butchering one another....
Commoners die by the tens of thousands,
White bones lie exposed in the wilds,
For hundreds of miles not a chicken squawks.
One in a hundred of the inhabitants survives.
Thinking of it wrenches your guts.

66 Cao Cao, *Works of Cao Cao,* probably compiled shortly after Cao Cao's death in 220 CE but lost and then reconstructed much later

The images of desolation were especially moving when the poem was chanted, as was the practice in Cao Cao's time.

In 196 CE—the same year that the imperial court moved back to the capital—Cao Cao finished conquering the Yellow Turbans. Cao was now so powerful that he, not the emperor, was in charge.

Cao Cao had his own ideas of what made a good leader. He wrote in another poem,

NOT ENOUGH FOR A POSITIVE I.D.

Cao Cao's facial hair must have looked unusual, because the only physical description of him that remains is that he had thin eyebrows and long sideburns.

Cao Cao, *Works of Cao Cao,* probably compiled shortly after Cao Cao's death in 220 CE but lost and then reconstructed much later

Of all the things between Heaven and Earth
Humans are to be prized.
Establish a lord to shepherd the people
And make rules for them.
The tracks of his chariots and horses
Criss-cross the empire.
He fires the stupid and promotes the bright;
The common people flourish.
Oh, excellent worthies and sages
Control the state.

Cao Cao wasn't just making pretty verse about how to lead—he really did try to be a good ruler. During his and his sons' reigns, the government put many reforms in place to improve life for a lot of people in China. He gave land to soldiers so that they could farm between battles, providing them with something useful to do and supplying food for the army. Unused farmland was given to homeless refugees, who then paid the government with part of their harvest, benefiting both the new landowners and the government. Cao Cao made the tax system more fair and passed a law forbidding wealthy landowners from taking over the property of the small farmers around them. He opened up employment in the court to anyone with talent, not just men with good reputations or family connections.

The Seven Sages, or wise men, of the Bamboo Grove (they used to meet in a bamboo grove to exchange poetry, song, and wine) were known not only for their skill at witty conversation, poetry, music, and art, but also for their enjoyment of drinking and partying.

Although many people were thrilled with these changes, others weren't so pleased. It's easy to imagine that the large landowners weren't happy to look at their neighbors' small farms and know that they couldn't just take the property, as had long been the custom. Many officials, who had been hoping to become important at court, resented the fact that men of greater ability were taking their places. And as always, some men thought that they, not Cao, should be in charge.

So Cao Cao spent the first 25 years of his rule putting down rebellions, fighting his enemies, and annexing territories. He unified northern China and took control of it, defeating several huge armies.

Two powerful warlords in south-central China felt threatened by Cao Cao's power and they united against him. In a battle on the central Yangzi, they set Cao's warships on fire and routed his army. Cao Cao himself escaped. One of the generals, Liu Bei, retained his hold on south-central China and even expanded his power westward.

Cao Cao died in 220 CE. Later generations admired his intelligence and boldness. To some people, though, the rise to power of this man of humble beginnings seemed almost too easy. The author of the 14th-century CE novel *Romance of the Three Kingdoms* showed him as a manipulative villain with magic powers. But whether he was good or evil, or some combination, Cao Cao, with his strong personality and great talents, held together the shaky remains of the once-powerful Han kingdom. For a long time after his death, no leader with anything approaching his abilities stepped forward, and the future of China looked uncertain.

The differences in the lives of the rich and the poor were still extreme, especially in the country. Zhongchang Tong described in the "Biography of Zhongchang Tong" in the History of the Later Han *the way his contemporaries showed off their wealth:*

*T*he mansions of the great landowners stretch in rows by the hundred, their opulent domains cover the whole countryside, their slaves can be counted by the thousand. ... The grandest houses are not big enough to contain all their jewels and gems; the hills and valleys are not wide enough to contain all the horses, oxen, sheep, and pigs. The splendid mansions are filled with ravishing boys and beautiful concubines; the halls within resound with the songs of singing girls and the music of courtesans.

The home of a wealthy person was more like a small village than a single house. Several related families and their servants all lived together, with one man being recognized as the head of the entire "household."

CHAPTER 22

A "BARBARIAN" LEADER
THE THREE KINGDOMS AND LIU YUAN

The strong leader Cao Cao always supported the Han emperor's right to rule China. But after he died in 220 CE, his son Cao Pi declared that he, not the Han ruler, was now the emperor. He called his new dynasty Wei, after the name of the central state of his kingdom. To make his claim to the throne more secure, Cao Pi married the two daughters of the former ruler.

Cao Pi had a serious rival: a general named Liu Bei, who had risen through the ranks in much the same way that Cao Cao had done. Liu Bei had earlier had some run-ins with Cao Cao from his base in south-central and western China where he ruled as emperor. In fact, by beating Cao Cao in a battle

THE THREE KINGDOMS, 230 CE

This Han battle scene from a tomb engraving proves that war horses were important not only for pulling chariots but also for enabling a mounted warrior to attack swiftly from above.

THE FALL OF THE HAN

184 CE
Yellow Turban rebellion

196 CE
Cao Cao controls
Northern China

215 CE
Zhang Lu and Daoists
surrender

220 CE
Cao Cao dies

221 CE
Liu Bei independent

222 CE
Sun Quan independent

263 CE
Han Dynasty falls

265 CE
Jin Dynasty established

280 CE
Wu falls

in 208 CE, Liu Bei prevented him from uniting the whole country. Liu Bei was related to a king of the Han dynasty and called his own dynasty Han. This made him popular in the eyes of some people who remembered the Han fondly and resented the way Cao Pi had set himself on the throne.

Meanwhile, in the fertile rice paddies around the mouth of the Yangzi River, a third power was forming. The powerful clans of the southeast came together around a man named Sun Quan. He was a younger son of a general and although his family was not very important, in 229 CE he declared himself Great Emperor of Wu.

So now there were three separate kingdoms—Wei, Han, and Wu—fighting over who should be in power. Followers of the three rulers—Cao Pi, Liu Bei, and Sun Quan—battled each other for many years. For a long time no one state could defeat the other two. Finally, in 263 CE, Cao Pi's successors managed to conquer Han, now run by Liu Bei's son. By then all political power in Wei was in the hands of a powerful family of generals called the Simas. Two years later a Sima overthrew the Wei and named his new state Jin. It took the state of Jin 15 years to conquer distant Wu and

THE MYSTERIOUS XIONGNU

The Chinese thought of the Xiongnu as a single people, but actually their empire included many ethnic groups. No one is sure just who the Xiongnu were. Some historians have suggested that they are related to modern Turkish people or to Mongols. Others think they were the ancestors of the Huns, or at least from the same ethnic group. Still other scholars think they were ancestors of a small group of people who live in the extreme northeastern corner of Siberia and speak languages we call Paleo-Siberian or Old Siberian.

finally put an end to the last of the Three Kingdoms.

It was clear that China needed someone of talent and energy to rule. Finally, in the fourth century CE, a "barbarian" named Liu Yuan rose from a tribe the Chinese considered uncivilized to become the ruler of a large and powerful state that threatened China's existence.

Like Liu Bei, Liu Yuan was distantly related to the family of the first Han emperor of China, but his father was the son of a leader of the Xiongnu, a non-Chinese tribe. General Cao Cao had allowed them to settle in China shortly before Liu Yuan was born. As was often the case, people later told stories about the leader that made it appear that there was something special about him even before he was born. They said that someone had told Liu Yuan's father that he had the look of a man who would bear great sons and grandsons. His mother had supposedly seen some strange things that indicated that a child of hers would be important. One was a dream in which a fish turned into a man and handed her a small object, saying, "This is the essence of the sun. Swallow it and you will give birth to a son destined for nobility." When the baby was born, the lines in his palm made a pattern that they read as the baby's name: **yuan**.

Yuan was a bright boy who studied the Chinese classics, history, and philosophy. He was good at martial arts, despite having an odd physique. According to his biography in the *Book of Jin*,

66 Fang Xuanling, *Book of Jin*, 644 CE

淵 }

A *yuan* is a deep pool or abyss.

66 Fang Xuanling, *Book of Jin*, 644 CE

He had arms as long as a gibbon's [a long-limbed ape] and was adept at archery; he was physically stronger than others. He was large and imposing of bearing, six feet three inches tall and with sideburns over three feet long. Just above his heart there were three red hairs, three feet six inches long.

A person like this would not escape notice for long. The emperor praised his intelligence and learning and thought he might be a good person to conquer the state of Wu (as it turns out, he wasn't involved in that particular war). But two of the emperor's ministers, worried about Liu Yuan's foreign heritage, warned him,

> If you give him power and authority, after he has sub-
> dued Wu, we fear he will not return. As the saying
> goes, "If he is not of our kind, his heart must be dif-
> ferent." Just leaving him in charge of his own divi-
> sion, we worry for Your Majesty.

Fang Xuanling, *Book of Jin,*
644 CE

Nomads on horses had a great advantage over soldiers who fought on foot.
The quilted padding on these attackers and their horses kept them warm and
helped protect them from their enemies' weapons.

Fang Xuanling, *Book of Jin*, 644 CE

Fang Xuanling, *Book of Jin*, 644 CE

Fang Xuanling, *Book of Jin*, 644 CE

Another minister warned that if Liu realized his own abilities, he would be hard to control. The minister said, "Once a dragon gets to fly among the clouds and rain, it can't be contained in a pond any longer."

But Liu was a popular leader. Leaders of the Xiongnu tribe thought that the Jin had lost the Mandate of Heaven, their divine right to rule, and that one of their own should take over. And who should be that one? Liu Yuan. "This is the time to establish a state and restore our enterprise," they said, as reported in the *Book of Jin*. "Liu Yuan surpasses all others in behavior and talent, and is more capable than anyone of the age."

Not surprisingly, he went along with their ideas, and added that as a member of the Liu family, which had founded the Han dynasty, he had a right to the throne. He said, "The Han possessed the empire for many long generations and their grace is intertwined in men's hearts.... I am a nephew of the Han clan, a sworn brother. Is it not proper, when an elder brother dies, for the younger to continue in his place?"

In 304 CE Liu Yuan became the first non-Chinese emperor of China, although he claimed that two famous rulers of the past, Yu the Great and King Wen, had also been from "barbarian" tribes. But he didn't enjoy his success for long. He died in 310 CE, after naming his son his heir. But the son was not as strong a ruler as his father had been, and the empire that Liu Yuan built soon crumbled.

CHAPTER 23

A FOREIGN GOD UNITES CHINA

BUDDHISM AFTER THE HAN

When the Han dynasty came to an end in 220 CE, so did Chinese unity. The Three Kingdoms that arose a few years later turned into 16 kingdoms in the next century, and borders and alliances continued to shift for hundreds of years. Most of the country was briefly reunited under a dynasty called the Western Jin, but these rulers undermined their own authority by giving large pieces of land to princes who then craved even more power.

Non-Chinese groups took advantage of the lack of central leadership to try to seize control of the government. For more than a century (304 to 439 CE), China was the site of almost constant warfare. Daily life was dangerous and unpredictable, and trade became nearly impossible. This made the country's financial situation shaky.

When non-Chinese rulers took over the northern part of China in 316 CE, millions of Chinese fled to the south. It must have been a shock to have to uproot their lives from the places where they had lived, usually for many generations. They found it especially difficult to leave the graves of their revered ancestors.

Northern China is mostly a dry, flat plain. The south is more mountainous, wet, and misty, and would not have seemed like home to the refugees. Mosquitoes thrived in the damp climate and many northerners died of malaria when they moved to the south. The newcomers also must have experienced culture

Guanyin is depicted as a Chinese man wearing Indian clothes, showing the way Buddhism combined and merged with local Chinese traditions. Guanyin is sometimes shown with 1,000 arms, symbolizing his multiple identities. In fact, he had so many different identities that he was later even worshiped as a female figure.

Foreigners looked very exotic to the Chinese. This foreign monk's beard and moustache are much thicker than those of most Chinese men, and his short hair and earring are also very un-Chinese. The scroll he is holding shows an Indian script, which makes sense, given that Buddhism originated in India.

shock. In the north, people either were native Chinese or had lived there for so long that they felt Chinese. But the south was home to many non-Chinese people with completely different languages, cultures, and customs. The newcomers had a lot to get used to.

Sometimes whole villages moved south. The settlers built new homes and often gave their new settlement the same name as the town they came from. They tried to preserve their old way of life as much as possible.

This move in 317 CE was only the latest in several waves of migration, although it was by far the largest. Earlier upper-class immigrants from the north had already established homes in the south.

The aristocrats in southern China didn't seem interested in helping the newcomers, but they were fascinated by a custom they brought with them, called "Pure Talk." They would gather to discuss philosophical questions and try to outdo each other in clever speech. An example of Pure Talk from the north, reported in *New Account of Tales of the World* of 430 CE, says:

66 Liu Yiqing, *New Account of Tales of the World*, 430 CE

When Wang Bi reached maturity he went to visit Pei Hui. Pei asked him, "If 'non-being' is truly the source of everything, why is it that the wise man Confucius never mentions it yet the *Laozi* talks about it incessantly?" Bi replied, "The sage embodied non-being, but non-being cannot be taught, so his words always focus on being. Laozi and Zhuangzi were still trapped in being, so they always taught about that which they lacked."

It's not hard to understand why ordinary people couldn't relate to these intellectuals.

Life was getting harder. Desperate poverty forced many people to sell themselves or their children into slavery. Those on the losing side of a battle would also find themselves enslaved, and slaves' lives were not seen as important. Slaves could even be beaten to death for no reason and the murderer would not have to worry about punishment.

So it's no wonder that most people lost their faith in their government—what government there was. They had also lost a feeling of unity with other Chinese. The people who had fled the north were angry and ashamed that they had been forced to leave the parts of China that had given birth to their earliest dynasties, the Shang and Zhou, and the lands that held the graves of these revered imperial ancestors and such important people as the philosopher Confucius. Even worse, their former home was under the control not just of foreigners, but of foreigners whom the Chinese considered uncivilized barbarians. What could fill this gap, giving people something to believe in and something to make them feel a sense of togetherness?

Surprisingly, the answer came from a source that had originally been foreign as well: the religion of Buddhism, which had been introduced in China centuries before. Many Chinese were initially suspicious of Buddhism, not only because of its foreign origin but also because some of its practices were strange to them. But many aspects of the religion appealed to people. Buddhists helped people in their daily lives. For instance, monasteries and convents gave refuge to people worn out from constant warfare and oppression. Monks and nuns performed charitable acts at a time when people felt abandoned by their government and other institutions. Women had a new opportunity: they

Floor-to-ceiling images of Buddhas and other divine figures cover the inside of a cave in Shanxi Province. Monks who lived in the complex used the caves as places for meditation.

OMNIVORES OR HERBIVORES?

Buddhists in China are vegetarians, although in many other parts of the world, they may eat meat. In fact, the Buddha himself was supposed to have died from eating bad pork.

could escape from their stressful lives by joining a convent.

Buddhism offered hope for the next world, too. Both women and men were encouraged to pursue salvation. And perhaps the most attractive idea was that reincarnation offered hope that anyone who lived a good life had a chance to be rewarded with a less-difficult existence in the future.

Still, it took a long time for Buddhism to become widely accepted. This process was finally given a boost when Emperor Wu of the Liang dynasty ascended the throne in 502 CE.

Emperor Wu converted to Buddhism as an adult, and like many converts, he was even more passionate about his new religion than some of the people who had been born into it. Three times he stepped down from the throne and entered the Buddhist order as a **novice** monk. Each time he entered the monastery, he took vows promising to stay there the rest of his life, so each time he left, the government had to pay a ransom to get him back. This clever tactic forced the government to give money, and the emperor's many other donations enriched the monasteries.

Wu's beliefs influenced the way he ruled. Buddhism forbids the taking of life, and Wu was reluctant to order executions and reduced the use of torture. In many cases he pardoned criminals rather than punishing them. He issued **edicts** encouraging people to enter monasteries and convents. He promoted vegetarianism and said that animals should not be killed even in sacrifices, a custom that went back centuries.

Chinese rulers had long claimed that they were so superior to everyone else that sitting in front of the emperor was a serious insult, even a crime. Wu showed his respect for Buddhist priests when he allowed one to remain seated in his presence. This symbolized the respect he had for the religion: the whole Buddhist order was outside the control of the imperial government. Later Buddhist texts speak of Bodhidharma, the legendary founder of Chan Buddhism, which emphasizes meditation over the study of texts. Chan Buddhism is better known in the West by its Japanese name, Zen. Bodhidharma came to China and met King Wu.

Buddhism became an important religion in China. Many of the most beautiful artworks, temples, and crafts in China were made by and for the worshippers of the Buddha, and his thoughts, as reinterpreted by his Chinese followers, shaped much of that country's thinking through the centuries. Buddhism changed in China, but Buddhism also changed China in many profound ways.

A novice is a person who enters a religious order, often making a lifelong commitment to the religious community. In many religions a novice must undergo a period of training before taking final vows.

An edict is a proclamation by a ruler that often has the force of law.

COMBATIVE BUGS

The Chinese martial art *gongfu*—better known in the West as Kung-fu—was supposedly created by Bodhidharma. It is said that he developed it after watching animals and insects fight.

EPILOGUE

One day in 1986, workers from a factory in Sanxingdui, in China's southwestern province of Sichuan, were digging clay for bricks when they found something much more precious: about a dozen ancient jade dagger-axes and carved tablets. Archaeologists immediately rushed to the site and in a few months they had carefully dug out two deep pits filled with ancient remains that dated from about 3000 years ago.

One pit contained over 400 objects, including elephant tusks that had been burned before being buried. The fact that they were burned makes scholars think that the tusks were offered to the gods, who could enjoy the smoke as it wafted up to them in the heavens. The archaeologists also found many clamshells, and bronze, ivory, and jade pieces.

The second pit held about 800 objects, including more than 60 tusks lying on top of objects made of bronze, jade, and stone. The bronze objects in this pit were astonishing, especially a life-size statue of a human. This was the earliest full-scale bronze human figure from China. The archaeologists also unearthed an eerie-looking bronze mask covered with **gold leaf**. Although scholars have not yet figured out exactly how these strange and beautiful figures were used, the fact that they look so different from real human beings led scholars to speculate that they were not intended to be realistic and were probably used in some kind of religious ritual.

What intrigued many scholars the most was that until 1986 nobody had any idea that this area had been important in the ancient history of China. Although the finds in the pit proved that the civilization that produced them was wealthy and powerful, with skilled artisans, no texts mentioned anything about the culture or its people. China is a huge country—about 3,696,100 square miles—and brickworkers digging in one small area that nobody thought was historically important accidentally found a fantastic treasure. So

Gold leaf is a layer of gold applied to a more solid background. Modern gold leaf is usually only about 4/1,000,000 of an inch thick.

Archaeologists carefully preserve a bowl unearthed from the site at Sanxingdui in Sichuan Province. By studying exactly where and in what position the pot lay, conditions of the soil around it, and other clues, they can piece together facts about the culture that produced it.

the odds are great that there are more hidden treasures lying around underground.

Some will soon be lying under water.

In 1994 the Chinese government began building the largest dam ever constructed, on the Yangzi River—the third-longest river in the world—near an area called the Three **Gorges**. The government hopes that the dam will protect the area downstream from disastrous flooding and will provide desperately needed electricity to the people in the region. Unfortunately, the lake that the dam will produce will also flood an enormous area.

Archaeologists scrambled into action. Yu Weichao, the director of China's National History Museum of China and head of the team working to save as many ancient artifacts as possible, reminded the world that "the sites in this area are too valuable to be lost.... Protecting cultural relics enhances everyone's understanding of ancient cultures."

A gorge is a ravine or narrow valley. The Yangzi River has cut deep gorges through the rocks in Sichuan and western Hubei provinces.

Before 1994, archaeologists had made finds in the Three Gorges area: artifacts dating back to the Paleolithic Age (more than 10,000 years ago), unique objects from the Neolithic (around 5000 to 2000 BCE), evidence of the extraordinary and little-known Ba civilization (about 2000 to 220 BCE), and other treasures. Chinese archaeologists begged the government to spend more money to speed up the process of uncovering as much of the precious past as they could before the huge reservoir (270 miles long) flooded it forever.

Instead, the budget was greatly reduced, from $250 million to $37.5 million. This might seem like a large amount of money until you consider the size and importance of the site.

Over the last decade, there has not been enough money to guard the digs adequately, and looters have made illegal digs and have stolen what they found. Finds from the Three Gorges area have turned up for auction around the world. While collectors may enjoy the beautiful artworks and interesting artifacts that they buy from illegal digs, archaeologists and historians have lost many chances to understand a large span of the history of this ancient and fascinating civilization.

Scholars think this bronze head wearing a gold mask found in Sichuan represents either a god or a deceased ruler from the Sanxingdui civilization from about 1000 BCE.

If all goes as planned, the Three Gorges dam will generate 85 billion kilowatt hours of electricity a year—one ninth of China's power. It will also stop the floods that have plagued the Chinese for centuries.

Fortunately, archaeologists and other scholars from all over the world are helping in the effort to rescue what they can before the dam is completed.

Scholars from different areas must work together to fit together the pieces of the puzzle of ancient Chinese history. For centuries, Chinese scholars have studied books written by their ancestors, and archaeological finds constantly turn up new meanings for passages of the texts and clear up puzzling sections. Working with both texts and artifacts, historians can reconstruct our ideas of the ancient Chinese world more accurately and realistically. Every generation produces people interested in the past and more precise methods of dealing with the information that they find. As archaeologists make more discoveries and work with historians and other scholars to interpret these discoveries, they will continue to uncover new aspects of the long history of China.

THE MYSTERIOUS BA

The people of the Ba civilization lived over a wide range of south western China, including the Three Gorges area that is now almost completely under water. They lived by fishing, hunting, and farming. They also made salt, a valuable trade good. Nobody knows where these mysterious people came from or what became of them and their civilization.

TIMELINE

The centuries BCE and CE are mirror images of each other. The years go backwards before the Year 1 CE. So someone born in 2000 BCE who died in 1935 BCE would have lived to be 65 years old. On both sides of the "mirror," the 200s can also be called the 3rd century, the 900s are called the 10th century, and so on—BCE as well as CE.

BCE

700,000–200,000
Peking Man lives near present-day Beijing

5000–4000
Hemudu culture settles and cultivates rice on Hangzhou Bay

5000–3000
Yangshao culture settles villages in the Yellow River valley in North China

3000–2000
Longshan culture builds walled cities, develops class society, makes fine black pottery on Shandong peninsula

ca. 1500–1046
Shang dynasty creates a bronze age empire in Northern China

1046
Zhou conquers Shang

1046–771
Western Zhou period

1046–221
Zhou dynasty rules China

781–771
King You rules; Western Zhou falls

770–476
Spring and Autumn Period

685–643
Duke Huan of Qi rules as hegemon

551–479
Confucius lives

475–221
Warring States period

433
Marquis of Zeng dies

403
Zhan, Han, and Wei divide state of Jin; era of the Warring States begins, according to some historians

about 370–290
Confucian philosopher
Mencius (Meng Ke) lives

369–286
Daoist philosopher
Zhuangzi lives

361–338
Shang Yang makes
reforms in Qin

256
Liu Bang born

246
Ying Zheng ascends throne as King of Qin

221
Qin conquers China, Ying Zheng becomes
Shi Huangdi, or First Emperor of China

211
Qin Shi Huangdi dies; General Zhao Gao
puts Huhai on throne

202
Liu Bang outmaneuvers Xiang Yu in
battle to become emperor and founds
Han dynasty

139–132
Han emperor Wu sends general to open
up trade through Central Asia and expand
Chinese influence

C E

9–23
Wang Mang becomes
first emperor of the
Xin dynasty

25
Liu Xiu restores
Han

65
First record of
Buddhism in China

142
Zhang Ling experiences
revelation,
founds Daoism

184
Yellow Turbans rebel in uprising

215
Cao Cao conquers the Celestial Master state

220
Cao Cao dies; Cao Pi founds Wei dynasty, the Three Kingdoms begin

263
Wei conquers Han state founded by Liu Bei in Sichuan

265
Jin dynasty of Sima family replaces Wei

280
Jin conquers Wu state founded by Sun Quan, unifying China

304
Liu Yuan establishes Xiongnu kingdom of Han

317
Xiongnu capture capital; Jin moves south to found Eastern Jin

502–549
Emperor Wu of Liang dynasty promotes Buddhism

589
Defeat of Chen dynasty in south leads to reunification of China

FURTHER READING AND WEBSITES

Entries with 💬 indicate primary source material.

GENERAL WORKS ON ANCIENT CHINA

Cotterell, Arthur. *Eyewitness: Ancient China.* New York: DK Publishing, 2000.

💬 d'Hormon, André, and Rémi Mathieu, trans. *"Guoyu": Propos sur les principautés,* vol. 2, *Zhouyu* Paris: Collège de France, Institut des Hautes Études Chinoises, 1985.

Ebrey, Patricia Buckley. *Cambridge Illustrated History of China.* New York: Cambridge University Press, 1996.

Fisher, Leonard Everett. *The Great Wall of China.* New York: Aladdin Library, 1995.

Hall, Eleanor J. *Ancient Chinese Dynasties.* San Diego, Calif.: Lucent Books, 2000.

💬 Karlgren, Bernhard, trans. *The Book of Odes.* Stockholm: Museum of Far Eastern Antiquities, 1950.

💬 ———, trans. *The Book of Documents.* Stockholm: Museum of Far Eastern Antiquities, 1950.

Levenson, Joseph R., and Franz Schurmann. *China: An Interpretive History, from the Beginnings to the Fall of Han.* Berkeley: University of California Press, 1969.

Major, John S. *The Silk Route: 7,000 Miles of History.* New York: HarperTrophy, 1996.

Mann, Elizabeth. *The Great Wall.* New York: Miyaka Press, 1997.

💬 Mather, Richard B., trans. *Shih-shuo Hsin-yü: A New Account of Tales of the World,* 2nd ed. Michigan Classics in Chinese Studies 95. Ann Arbor, 2002.

Murowchick, Robert E., ed. *Cradles of Civilization: China.* Norman: University of Oklahoma Press, 1994.

Rawson, Jessica, ed. *Mysteries of Ancient China.* New York: George Braziller, 1996.

💬 Roberts, Moss. *Romance of the Three Kingdoms: A Historical Novel.* Abridged, Berkeley: University of California Press, 1991.

💬 ———. *Three Kingdoms: China's Epic Drama.* New York: Pantheon, 1976.

Shaughnessy, Edward L., ed. *China: Empire and Civilization.* New York: Oxford University Press, 2000.

Time-Life Books. *China's Buried Kingdoms.* Alexandria, Va.: Time-Life Books, 1993.

💬 Waley, Arthur, trans. *The Book of Songs: The Ancient Chinese Classic of Poetry.* Ed. Joseph R. Allen. New York: Grove, 1996.

💬 Watson, Burton, trans. *Records of the Grand Historian: Qin Dynasty,* by Sima Qian. New York: Columbia University Press, 1993.

💬 ———, trans. *The Tso chuan: Selections from China's Oldest Narrative History.* New York: Columbia University Press, 1989.

ATLASES

Blunden, Caroline, and Mark Elvin, eds. *Cultural Atlas of China.* New York: Checkmark Books, 1998.

Haywood, John. *World Atlas of the Past, Vol. 1: The Ancient World.* New York: Oxford University Press, 1999.

DICTIONARIES AND ENCYCLOPEDIAS

Hook, Brian, ed. *Cambridge Encyclopedia of China.* Cambridge: Cambridge University Press, 1982.

Perkins, Dorothy. *Encyclopedia of China: The Essential Reference to China, Its History and Culture.* New York: Facts on File, 1999.

ARCHAEOLOGY

Bishop, Kevin, and Simon Holledge. *Xi'an: China's Ancient Capital, Third Edition.* Union Lake, Mich.: Odyssey Publications, 2000.

Childs-Johnson, Elizabeth, et al. "Race Against Time," *Archaeology* Nov./Dec., 1996: 38–43.

Cotterell, Arthur. *The First Emperor of China: The Story Behind the Terracotta Army of Mount Li.* New York: Penguin, 1988.

Hessler, Peter. "The New Story of China's Ancient Past," *National Geographic,* July 2003: 56–81.

Zich, Arthur. "China's Three Gorges Before the Flood," *National Geographic,* Sept. 1997: 2–33.

BIOGRAPHY

Dawson, Raymond S. *Confucius.* New York: Oxford University Press, 1984.

Levi, Jean. *The Chinese Emperor,* trans. Barbara Bray. New York: Vintage Books, 1989.

HAN DYNASTY

[66] Dubs, Homer H., trans. *The History of the Former Han Dynasty,* by Ban Gu. 3 vols. Baltimore: Waverly, 1938-55.

Edwards, Mike. "Han Dynasty: A Chinese Empire to Rival Rome," *National Geographic,* Feb. 2004: 2–29.

Immell, Myra. *The Han Dynasty.* Farmington Hills, Mich.: Greenhaven, 2002.

Loewe, Michael. *Everyday Life in Early Imperial China during the Han Period, 202 B.C.–A.D. 220.* New York: Putnam, 1968.

[66] Watson, Burton, trans. *Records of the Grand Historian: Han Dynasty,* by Sima Qian. Rev. ed. 2 vols. New York: Columbia University Press, 1993.

MYTHOLOGY AND ANCIENT STORIES

Birch, Cyril. *Tales from China.* New York, Oxford University Press, 2001.

Birrell, Anne. *Chinese Mythology: An Introduction.* Baltimore and London: Johns Hopkins University Press, 1993.

The Ch'i-lin Purse: Collection of Ancient Chinese Stories. Retold by Linda Fang. New York: Farrar Straus and Giroux, 1995.

Roberts, Moss, trans. *Chinese Fairy Tales and Fantasies.* New York: Pantheon, 1979.

Sanders, Tao Tao Liu. *Dragons, Gods and Spirits from Chinese Mythology.* New York: Schocken, 1982.

PHILOSOPHY

[66] Legge, James, trans. *The Sacred Books of China: The Texts of Confucianism.* 4 vols. Oxford: Clarendon Press, 1879–85.

[66] ———, trans. *The Chinese Classics,* 2nd ed. 5 vols. 1893–95. Reprint, Taipei: SMC, 1991.

[66] Mei, Yi-pao, trans. *The Ethical and Political Works of Motse.* Probsthain's Oriental Series 19. London, 1929.

[66] Rickett, W. Allyn, trans. *Political, Economic, and Philosophical Essays from Early China,* 2nd ed. Boston and Worcester, Mass.: Cheng and Tsui, 2001.

Sawyer, Ralph D., trans. *The Seven Military Classics of Ancient China: History and Warfare.* Boulder, Colo.: Westview, 1993.

[66] Waley, Arthur, trans. *The Analects of Confucius.* London: George Allen & Unwin, 1938.

———. *Three Ways of Thought in Ancient China.* London: George Allen & Unwin, 1939.

———. *The Way and Its Power: A Study of the Tao Tê Ching and Its Place in Chinese Thought.* UNESCO Collection of Representative Works—Chinese Series. New York: Grove Weidenfeld, 1958.

RELIGION

Bokenkamp, Stephen R., trans. "Commands and Admonitions for the Families of the Great Dao." In *Early Daoist Scriptures,* 149–185. Berkeley: University of California Press, 1997.

Foltz, Richard C. *Religions of the Silk Road: Overland Trade and Cultural Exchange from Antiquity to 1500 BC.* New York: Palgrave Macmillan, 2000.

Henricks, Robert G., trans. *Lao Tzu's Tao Te Ching: A Translation of the Startling New Documents Found at Guodian.* New York: Columbia University Press, 2000.

———, trans. *Lao-tzu: Te-tao ching. A New Translation Based on the Recently Discovered Ma-wang-tui Texts.* New York: Ballantine, 1989.

Waley, Arthur, trans. *The Way and Its Power: A Study of the Tao Tê Ching and Its Place in Chinese Thought.* New York: Grove Weidenfeld, 1958.

Ware, James R., trans. *Alchemy, Medicine, and Religion in the China of A.D. 320: The Nei P'ien of Ko Hung (Pao-p'u tzu).* Cambridge, Mass.: MIT Press, 1996. Reprint, Mineola, N.Y.: Dover, 1981.

Whitfield, Susan. *Life Along the Silk Road.* Berkeley: University of California Press, 2001.

Wood, Frances. *The Silk Road: Two Thousand Years in the Heart of Asia.* Berkeley: University of California Press, 2003.

SCIENCE AND TECHNOLOGY

Beshore, George W. *Science in Ancient China.* New York: Orchard Books, 1998.

Temple, Robert. *The Genius of China: 3,000 Years of Science, Discovery, and Invention.* New York: Simon & Schuster, 1986.

Unschuld, Paul. *Chinese Medicine.* Brookline, Mass.: Paradigm Publications, 1998.

Williams, Suzanne, and Andrea Fong. *Made in China: Ideas and Inventions from Ancient China.* Berkeley, Calif.: Pacific View Press, 1997.

WARFARE

Ames, Roger T., trans. *Sun-tzu: The Art of Warfare. The First English Translation Incorporating the Recently Discovered Yin-ch'üeh-shan Texts.* New York: Ballantine, 1993

Hessler, Peter. "Chasing the Wall: China's Great Wall," *National Geographic,* January 2003: 2–33.

Peers, Chris. *Ancient Chinese Armies 1500–200 BC.* Northants, England: Osprey Publications, 1990.

———. *Imperial Chinese Armies 200 BC–589 AD.* Northants, England: Osprey Publications, 1995.

———. *Warlords of China, 700 B.C. to A.D. 1662.* New York: Sterling, 1998.

WOMEN

Ebrey, Patricia Buckley. *Women and the Family in Chinese History.* London: Routledge, 2002.

Swann, Nancy Lee. *Pan Chao, Foremost Woman Scholar of China, First Century A.D.: Background, Ancestry, Life, and Writings of the Most Celebrated Chinese Woman of Letters.* New York: Russell & Russell, 1968, first ed. 1932.

WEBSITES

Appreciation of the Art of Chinese Calligraphy
www.chinapage.org/calligraphy.html
An introduction to the principles of Chinese calligraphy with several examples of calligraphy by famous artists.

The Art of the Chinese Bronze
www.chinavoc.com/arts/handicraft/bronze.htm
A Chinese site with basic information on the ancient Chinese bronze industry.

Asia for Educators
http://afe.easia.columbia.edu
Provides links to Asian Studies websites
across the United States.

AskAsia: A K-12 Resource of The Asia Society
www.AskAsia.org
Links to references and guides for both students and teachers.

**Buddhist Studies: Buddha Dharma Education
Association & Buddhanet**
*www.buddhanet.net/e-learning/buddhistworld/
china-txt.htm*
A simple history of Buddhism in China with
links to a timeline of Buddhism and illustrated
lists of Chinese gods and festivals.

Buddhist Studies WWW Virtual Library
www.ciolek.com/WWWVL-Buddhism.html
An excellent collection of links about all different aspects of Buddhism, with contribu-
tions from top scholars.

China
*www.cmi.k12.il.us/Urbana/projects/AncientCiv/
china.html*
Website on ancient China created by sixth and
seventh grade students in Illinois.

China for Kids
www.gigglepotz.com/china.htm
This site provides a basic introduction to
many aspects of Chinese history, culture, and
society oriented to schoolkids.

Chinese Musical Instruments
www.bigskymusic.com/b-world.htm
Introduces the four classes of Chinese musical
instrument: bowed strings, plucked strings,
winds, and percussion.

Classical Chinese Furniture
www.chinese-furniture.com
A well-illustrated site by Curtis Evarts that
gives an overview of traditional Chinese furniture and introduces one piece in depth.

**Condensed China: Chinese History for
Beginners**
www.asterius.com/china/
This site provides short overviews of the
major periods in Chinese history.

Encyclopedia: Chinese Minorities
*www.nationmaster.com/encyclopedia/Chinese-
minorities*
This site gives an overview of the ethnic
minorities in China with detailed links on the
culture and history of some of the groups.

History of China
www-chaos.umd.edu/history/toc.html
This is a full history of China online, with a
strong emphasis on events after 1842.

The International Dunhuang Project
http://idp.bl.uk/
The British Library provides the best introduction to the texts and images found at
Dunhuang, which date to 500–1000 CE.

Romance of Three Kingdoms
www.threekingdoms.com
This site provides an introduction to the novel
Romance of the Three Kingdoms and a full
translation of the novel.

The Taoist Tradition: A Historical Outline
*www.uga.edu/religion/rk/basehtml/guides/
TMGID.html*
A detailed outline of the development of
Daoism, linking philosophical Daoism and
religious Daoism.

A Visual Sourcebook for Chinese Civilization
http://depts.washington.edu/chinaciv
This site from a top scholar has informative
and well-illustrated pages on ancient tombs,
Buddhism, calligraphy, and military technology.

INDEX

A QUICK GUIDE TO PRONUNCIATION

ai	the y in fry	hai is pronounced hi
an	the on in on	fan is pronounced fahn
ang	the ong in gong	fang is pronounced fahng
ao	the ow in cow	gao is pronounced gaow
c	the ts in fits	cao is pronounced tsaow
e	the oo in foot	se is pronounced suh
ei	the ay in bay	fei is pronounced fay
en	the un in fun	men is pronounced muhn
eng	the ung in fungus	meng is pronounced muhng
er	the are in are	mu'er is pronounced moo-er
g	the g in girl	gao is pronounced haow
i	the ee in glee	qi is pronounced chee
i (after c, ch, s, sh, z, zh)	the r in sure	shi is pronounced shur
ia	the ea in caveat	xia is pronounced sheeah
iang	ee, plus the yang in yang	chiang is pronounced cheeahng
ie	ee, plus the yeah in yeah	qie is pronounced cheeyeh
in	the ee in been	xin is pronounced sheen
iu	ee, plus the ow in blow	jiu is pronounced jeeoh
o	the aw in awful	mo is pronounced mwoh
ou	oh	zhou is pronounced jo
q	the ch in child	qin is pronounced cheen

u	the ew in few	yu is pronounced yew
u	the oo in boo	gu is pronounced goo
ua	the wa in water	hua is pronounced hwah
uan	the wan in wander	huan is pronounced hwahn
uan	oo, plus the en in men	quan in pronounced chooen
uang	the wan in wander plus ng	huang is pronounced hwahng
ue	oo, plus the e in went	que is pronounced chooeh
un	the won in won	sun is pronounced swun
uo	the awe in awful	guo is pronounced gwoh
x	the sh in should	xing is pronounced shing
yuan	oo, plus the en in went	yuan is pronounced yewen
z	the ds in yards	zeng is pronounced dzeng
zh	the j in juice	zhou is pronounced jo

TEXT CREDITS

Works cited not in English have been translated by Terry Kleeman.

MAIN TEXT

p. 18: Clarke, Samuel. *Among the Tribes in South-West China*. London: China Inland Mission, Morgan and Scott, 1911.

p. 48: Shima Kunio, *Inkyo bokuji sōrui* (Tokyo: Kyuko, 1977), 82, 479b.

p. 54: *Shijing* (Harvard-Yenching Index ed.), 59/236/8.

p. 55: *Shangshu*, "Jinteng" (Harvard-Yenching Index ed.), 13/26/0424.

p. 56: *Shangshu*, "Jiugao," 15/30/426.

p. 59: Sima Qian, *Shiji* (Beijing: Zhonghua shuju punctuated ed.), 4/142.

p. 61: *Zuozhuan* (Harvard-Yenching Index ed.), 56/Zhuang 9/7.

p. 62: *Zuozhuan*, 56/Zhuang 9/7.

p. 63: Confucius, *Analects* (Harvard-Yenching Index ed.), 28/14/17.

p. 64: *Guoyu*, "Jinyu 1" (Shanghai: Shanghai guji chubanshe, 1978), 7/252–3.

p. 65: *Guoyu*, "Jinyu 1," 7/252–3.

p. 67: *Guoyu*, "Jinyu 1," 7/252–3; *Shijing*, Mao 209, 51/209/2.

p. 68: *Guoyu*, "Jinyu 1," 7/252–3.

p. 69: *Guoyu*, "Jinyu 2," 8/289, 8/291–2.

p. 76: Confucius, *Analects* (Harvard-Yenching Index ed.), 1/1/1.

p. 78: Confucius, *Analects*, 2/1/16, 22/12/2, 12/2/6.

p. 79: Confucius, *Analects*, 1/1/3.

p. 80: Confucius, *Analects*, 2/7/19.

p. 81: Chen Qiyou, ed., *Lüshi Chunqiu jiaoshi* (Shanghai: Xuelin, 1984), 19/1257.

p. 82: Sima Qian, "Biography of Laozi," 63/ 2140.

p. 83: Sima Qian, "Biography of Laozi," 63/ 2140.

p. 86: Laozi, *Daodejing,* chapters 56, 37.

p. 88: Laozi, *Daodejing*, chapters 56, 37; Laozi, *Daodejing,* chapters 3, 61.

p. 91: *Sunzi,* chapters 1–3.

p. 95: Sima Qian, *Shiji*, 5/205.

p. 96: Sima Qian, *Shiji*, 6/230.

p. 97: Sima Qian, *Shiji*, 6/265.

p. 98: Sima Qian, *Shiji*, 6/265.

p. 102: Ban Gu, *Hanshu* (Beijing: Zhonghua shuju punctuated edn.), 1B/80; 1B/26.

p. 103: Sima Qian, *Shiji*, 7/336.

p. 104: Ban Gu, *Hanshu,* 1B/80; 1B/26.

p. 105: Ban Gu, *Hanshu,* 1A/44; Sima Qian, *Shiji,* 7/336.

p. 109: Ouyang Xun, ed., *Yiwen Leiju* (Shanghai: Zhonghua shuju, 1965), 30/538.

p. 110: *Shijing*, 36/167/1.

p. 111: Ban Gu, *Hanshu*, 45/2171.

p. 112: Fan Ye, *Hou Hanshu* (Beijing: Zhonghua shuju punctuated edn.), 84/2786–2791.

p. 114: Fan Ye, *Hou Hanshu*, 84/2786-2791, 28B/962–978.

p. 115: Fan Ye, *Hou Hanshu*, 84/2786–791.

p. 116: Fan Ye, *Hou Hanshu*, 84/2786–791.

p. 117: Fan Ye, *Hou Hanshu*, 28B/962–978.

p. 119: Mozi, *Mozi*, 50/93/1.

p. 120: Lu You, *Jiannanji* (Sibu congkan edn.) 36.8; *Lu Fangweng quanji* (Hong Kong: Guangzhi shuju,), vol. 2, p. 556; Mao Yuanyi, *Wubeizhi* (1621 edn.), 105/17b–18a.

p. 124: Ban Gu, *Hanshu*, 69/4039–98.

p. 125: Ban Gu, *Hanshu*, 69/4039–98.

p. 126: Ban Gu, *Hanshu*, 69/4039–98.

p. 127: Ban Gu, *Hanshu*, 69/4039–98.

p. 129: Ban Gu, *Hanshu*, 69/4039–98.

p. 130: Ge Hong, *Shenxianzhuan*, quoted in Li Fang, ed., *Taiping guangji* (Beijing: Zhonghu shuju, 1961) 8.3.

p. 132: Ge Hong, *Shenxianzhuan,* quoted in Li Fang, ed., *Taiping guangji* (Beijing: Zhonghu shuju, 1961), 8.3.

p. 133: *Nüqing guilü* (Daoist canon, HY 789), 5/1a.

p. 134: Fan Ye, *Hou Hanshu,* 30B/1082.

p. 136: Ban Gu, *Hanshu,* 96A/3888–90.

p. 138: Fan Ye, *Hou Hanshu,* 30B/1082.

p. 140: Chen Shou, *Record of the Three Kingdoms,* 297.

p. 141: Cao Pi, *Essay on the Classics,* about 220 CE; "Duguan shan," Cao Cao, *Works of Cao Cao,* Huang Jie, ed., *Wei wudi shizhu* (Taipei: Shijie shuju, 1973), 6–7.

p. 142: "Haoli xing," Cao Cao, *Works of Cao Cao,* 10.

p. 146: Fang Xuanling, *Jinshu* (Beijing: Zhonghua Shuju edn.), 101/2644–54.

p. 147: Fang Xuanling, *Jinshu,* 101/2644–54.

p. 148: Fang Xuanling, *Jinshu,* 101/2644–54.

p. 150: Yang Yong, *Shishuo xinyu jiaojian* (Hong Kong: Dazhong shuju, 1969), 4.8, p. 152.

SIDEBARS

p. 106: Sima Qian, *Shiji,* Annals of Emperor Gaozu, 8/389.

p. 143: Chen Shou, *Hou Hanshu,* Biography of Zhongchang Tong, 49/1648. Balazs, Etienne. *Chinese Civilization and Bureaucracy.* New Haven, Conn.: Yale University Press, 1964, 219–220.

PICTURE CREDITS

Courtesy of the Institute of History and Philology, Academia Sinica: 38; Art Resource, NY: 35; The Avery Brundage Collection, B60B1034. © Asian Art Museum of San Francisco. Used by permission: 134; Banpo Museum: 28; By permission of The British Library Or. 2231: 104, Or. 7694: 37, Or 15333.e.1: 141, Or. 5896: 117, Or. 8210/S. 6825: 133; © Copyright The British Museum: 87, 128; © The Trustees of The British Museum: 139; Cambridge University Press: 42; Photograph by William Macquitty, Camera Press London: 129; Champion Shenblu Checker Chip: 23; © Christopher Liu/ChinaStock: 122; Attributed to Liang Kai, Chinese, early 13th century, Southern Song dynasty. *Sericulture.* Handscroll, ink and light color on paper, 26.5 x 98.5 cm. © The Cleveland Museum of Art, John L. Severance Fund, 1977.5: 119; "The Lun Yun," Published by Confucius Publishing Co. Ltd.: 76; © 2004 Cultural Relics Publishing House: cover, 24, 26, 29, 33, 43, 70, 72, 73, 96, 121, 142, 156; © Dunhuang Academy/Lois Connor: 147; Erich Lessing/Art Resource, NY: 75, 102; Field Museum Library Photo Archives, A108893_19: 85; Freer Gallery of Art, Smithsonian Institution Washington, D.C.: Gift of Charles Lang Freer, F.1911.24: 149; Freer Gallery of Art, Smithsonian Institution, Washington, D.C.: Purchase, F1936.6: 47; Hubei Provincial Museum: 60, 61, 74, 93; Library of Congress: 14; The Metropolitan Museum of Art, Ex coll.: C.C. Wang Family, From the P.Y. and Kinmay W. Tang Family Collection, Gift of the Oscar L. Tang Family, 1996. (1996.479a-c) Photograph by Malcom Varon. Photograph © 1991 The Metropolitan Museum of Art: 67; The Metropolitan Museum of Art, Gift of Mrs. Edward S. Harkness, 1947. (47.81.1) Photograph © 1995 The Metropolitan Museum of Art: 56; The Minneapolis Institute of Arts, Gift of Alan and Dena Naylor in memory of Thomas E. Leary: 126; MOA Museum of Art: 83; Robert Murowchick: 50; The Nelson-Atkins Museum of Art, Kansas City, Missouri (Purchase: Nelson Trust) 33-521/ Robert Newcombe: 143, 41-33/Orville Crane: 65; Photograph © 2004 Museum of Fine Arts, Boston: 123, 131; National Palace Museum, Taiwan, Republic of China: 11, 16, 115, 132, 150; © The Natural History Museum, London: 19, 21; Raymond Gehman/National Geographic Image Collection:111; O. Louis Mazzatenta/National Geographic Image Collection: 94, 99; Jade Knife, Hardinge Collection, 1960.1814, The Oriental Museum, University of Durham: 34; Osaka Municipal Museum of Art: 110; © Dermot Tatlow/Panos Pictures: 109; Photofest NYC:100; © Phototheque des Musees de la Ville de Paris/ Degraces: 49; John Reader/Photo Researchers, Inc.: 36; Princeton University Art Museum. Far Eastern Collection. Photo Credit: Bruce M. White. © 2003/2004 Photo: Trustees of Princeton University: 145; Réunion des Musées Nationaux/Art Resource, NY: 2, 80, 113; Arthur M. Sackler Gallery, Smithsonian Institution, Washington, D.C.: Gift of Arthur M. Sackler, S1987.482: 63; Image courtesy of *The Arthur M. Sackler Museum of Art and Archaeology at Peking University,* Beijing, China.www.sackler.org: 68; © Xinhua/Sovfoto: 15, 22, 118, 137, 155, 157; © Tianlong Jiao: 46; TravelChinaGuide.com: 31, 89, 91; © Inga Spence/Visuals Unlimited: 74; Werner Forman/Art Resource, NY: 152; © WorldArt Image Database: 45, 48; Yale University Press: 30, 32, 40, 54

TRACY BARRETT is the author of numerous books and magazine articles for young readers. A grant from the National Endowment for the Humanities to study medieval women writers inspired her award-winning young-adult novel *Anna of Byzantium*. Her most recent publications are *On Etruscan Time* and *The Ancient Greek World* (with Jennifer T. Roberts), also in the World in Ancient Times series. Tracy Barrett is Regional Advisor for the Midsouth with the Society of Children's Book Writers and Illustrators. She teaches courses on writing for children and on children's literature and makes presentations to students, librarians, and teachers. She is on the faculty of Vanderbilt University in Nashville, Tennessee, where she lives with her husband and two teenagers.

TERRY KLEEMAN is Associate Professor of Chinese and Religious Studies at the University of Colorado at Boulder. His research has taken him to Taisho University in Tokyo, the École Pratique des Hautes Études in Paris, and the Oriental Institute of Tokyo University. He is the author of *A God's Own Tale: The Book of Transformations of Wenchang the Divine Lord of Zitong* and *Great Perfection: Religion and Ethnicity in a Chinese Millennial Kingdom*. He has served since 2002 as President of the Society for the Study of Chinese Religions and is Managing Editor of *Studies in Central and East Asian Religions*.

RONALD MELLOR, who is professor of history at UCLA, first became enthralled with ancient history as a student at Regis High School in New York City. He is the statewide faculty advisor of the California History–Social Science Project (CHSSP), which brings university faculty together with K-12 teachers at sites throughout California. In 2000, the American Historical Association awarded the CHSSP the Albert J. Beveridge Award for K-12 teaching. Professor Mellor has held fellowships from the National Endowment for the Humanities and the American Council of Learned Societies. His research has centered on ancient religion and Roman historiography. His books include *Theia Rhome: The Goddess Roma in the Greek World*, *From Augustus to Nero: The First Dynasty of Imperial Rome*, *Tacitus*, *Tacitus: The Classical Heritage*, *The Historians of Ancient Rome* (with Marni McGee), *The Roman Historians*, and *The Ancient Roman World*, also in the World in Ancient Times series.

AMANDA PODANY is a specialist in the history of the Ancient Near East and a professor of history at California State Polytechnic University, Pomona. She has taught there since 1990 and is currently serving as the director of the university's honors program. From 1993 to 1997 she was executive director of the California History–Social Science Project, a professional development program for history–social science teachers at all grade levels. Her publications include *The Land of Hana: Kings, Chronology, Scribal Tradition*, and *The Ancient Near Eastern World* (with Marni McGee), also in the World in Ancient Times series. Professor Podany has also published numerous journal articles on ancient Near Eastern history and on approaches to teaching. She lives in Los Angeles with her husband and two children.